Bob McDonald
and Eric Grace

Illustrated by Bob Binks
and Gary Pearson

CBC Enterprises

Published by CBC Enterprises/Les Entreprises Radio-Canada, a division of the Canadian Broadcasting Corporation, P.O. Box 500, Station A, Toronto, Ontario M5W 1E6.

Canadian Cataloguing in Publication Data
McDonald, Bob, 1951-
    Wonderstruck

ISBN 0-88794-337-3

1. Science - Experiments - Juvenile literature.
I. Grace, Eric, 1948-   . II. CBC Enterprises.
III. Title.

Q164.M22 1988   j502'.8   C88-093352-6

Editor: Carl Heimrich
Design: Michael Solomon
Electronic Page Make-up: Allen Shechtman,
    Silver Bullet Productions

Distributed to the trade by
    The Canadian Book Marketing Group Ltd.

Printed and bound in Canada by
    John Deyell Company

1 2 3 4 5 6 7 / 94 93 92 91 90 89 88

Front Cover: Bob McDonald on roller skates, demonstrating Isaac Newton's principle of action-reaction. For a fuller explanation, see pages 13-14.

Back Cover: The "Water Parfait" experiment found on page 34. Experimenters (left to right): Guy Aspler, Nikisha Reyes, and Alice Manguel.

Special thanks to Liz Fox, Executive Producer of "Wonderstruck" for her assistance in the development of this project; to Lesley Williams for doing the research; and to Jonathon Neville for his comments on an early draft.

Table of Contents

Introduction

The hardest thing to do in science is ask good questions. That's why we turned to you. The questions in this book were chosen out of the hundreds of letters from viewers who watch "Wonderstruck" on TV. Looking for explanations, we found the most challenging questions are the simple ones. Since the questions came from you, we are giving you a chance to discover the answers yourselves in your own kitchens. By doing the Kitchen Demos, you become scientists, performing experiments in the laboratory to understand principles at work in nature. But don't be fooled by the simplicity of the Demos. After experimenting, a scientist thinks about the results and where else they might apply. That's what the "Did You Know?" sections are all about. These amazing facts show other places where the principles in the Demos are at work. It's fascinating to know that a simple effect, such as your shower curtain bending in when you turn on the shower, is the same effect that helps keep a jumbo jet in the air.

Thank you all for the great questions! Have fun discovering the answers!

Why does water boil at a lower temperature on top of a mountain

Getting water to boil depends only partly on adding heat. The actual temperature at which water boils also depends on the air pressure around the water.

Imagine a saucepan of water sitting on your stove. When you heat the water, some of it starts to turn into steam and escape into the air. As the water gets hotter, more steam appears. The air around the saucepan, however, is pressing down on the water's surface. This air pressure resists the upward pressure created by the escaping steam. Before the water can boil, the pressure of the steam must get high enough to equal the air pressure on the water's surface. At this point, the water won't get any hotter. Adding more heat just turns the rest of the water into steam.

Because the boiling point of water is affected by air pressure as well as by temperature, you can change the boiling point by changing the air pressure. That is what happens when you travel upwards from sea level. As you go higher, the air pressure becomes lower. With less air pressure, the water needs less heat to reach the boiling point.

This fact can make life uncomfortable for a mountaineer. When the kettle boils for tea or soup on a mountain, the water will only be lukewarm. On high mountains, you cannot make water hot enough to cook rice properly. And if you bake a cake on a mountain, you must add more water to the cake mix, or the cake will dry out before it is cooked. The cake will also rise higher in the

low air pressure and be in great danger of collapsing!

Does it surprise you to know that air has pressure? Air pushes in all directions – up and sideways as well as down. You can see the strength of air pressure in these two experiments.

A. The Amazing Glass

Things you need
- drinking glass
- piece of stiff cardboard, slightly larger than the top of the glass

What to do
1. Fill the glass right to the top with water.
2. Carefully slide the flat piece of cardboard across the rim of the glass. Make sure there is no air trapped between the water and the cardboard.
3. Hold the cardboard tightly against the glass with one hand and turn the glass

upside down over a sink or plastic pail.
4. Take your hand away from the cardboard.

Explanation
The pressure of the air pushing against the cardboard is greater than the force produced by the weight of the water in the glass. The cardboard will stay in place as long as it does not get soggy and start to sag.

B. The Shrinking Bottle

Things you need
- plastic jug with a tight screw-on top
- boiling water

✚ **SAFETY FIRST!** Be careful! Boiling water burns!

What to do
1. Carefully pour boiling water into the plastic jug until it is about a quarter full.
2. Screw the top on loosely and shake the jug until it is full of steam.
3. Tighten the top and run cold water over the jug. The sides of the jug will collapse inward.
4. Now loosen the top gradually and see what happens.

Explanation
When the steam inside the jug is suddenly cooled, it turns from steam into water. This lowers the pressure inside the jug. The higher air pressure on the outside of the jug pushes against the sides and crushes the jug. When you loosen the top, air rushes in and the jug springs back to its original shape.

DID YOU KNOW ???

- At the peak of Mount Everest, which rises more than three-quarters of the way upwards through the Earth's atmosphere, water boils at 55°C (131°F)!

- The planet Mars has very little atmosphere, and the air pressure on Mars is very low. You could boil water on Mars with the heat from your hand!
- One reason why astronauts wear pressurized spacesuits is to keep their blood from boiling in the low pressure of space.

- The Eiffel Tower in Paris weighs less than a column of air the same size.

What makes a spaceship rise

A spaceship is launched into the air by the force of expanding hot gases, which rush from the exhaust nozzle at the rear of the spaceship as fuel inside the spaceship is burned.

Spaceship fuel itself can be either solid or liquid. The most common fuel is a mixture of liquid oxygen and liquid hydrogen. These two liquids are kept in separate tanks inside the spaceship until the moment of launch. When the spaceship is ready to fire, the two liquids are combined inside a combustion chamber and burned.

If you have ever seen a film of a spaceship being launched, or have been lucky enough to see a launching in person, you will have noticed that spectacular clouds of vapour swirl around the spaceship's base. These clouds are made of the gases that are produced when the liquid fuel is burned. The gases expand inside the combustion chamber and then rush from the rocket at supersonic speed through the only opening available – the exhaust nozzle. The force of the gases rushing in one direction sends the spaceship in the opposite direction.

Rocket Race

You can see the force that sends rockets into space by making your own rocket with a balloon.

Things you need
- balloon
- drinking straw
- masking tape
- string, about 5 m (16.5 ft) long

What to do
1. Cut a piece of drinking straw about 5 cm (2 in) long, and thread the string through it.
2. Tie each end of the string to a heavy piece of furniture (or to two trees outside), making sure the string is tight and level.
3. Blow up the balloon, and tape it onto the straw at one end of the string, while holding the balloon's mouth squeezed shut.

You can feel for yourself the force that sends a spacecraft into the air if you throw a heavy weight while standing on roller skates. As you throw the weight in one direction, you are moved in the other.

4. Release the balloon and watch it go! Try timing it. You might want to compare the speeds of different balloons, or have a balloon race with friends.

Explanation

The movement of the balloon is caused by the air inside it rushing out in the opposite direction. The thrust does not depend, as some people think, on the jet of air pushing against the surrounding air. That is why rockets can work in airless outer space.

DID YOU KNOW ???

- The physical principle on which rocket propulsion is based was first described in 1687 by Isaac Newton. He showed that for every action there is an equal and opposite reaction.

- When any liquid is heated and converted into a gas, it expands to take up more room. You can see this when you boil a kettle or run a bath. The steam produced by the small amount of hot water in your kettle or tub is enough to fill the whole room.

- You can see a good demonstration of Newton's principle in shotguns and cannons. The reaction to the action of the bullet or cannon-ball being fired is kickback. Watch for the recoil of big guns in films about war.

- Fireworks are sent upwards in the same way as rockets. Gunpowder inside them burns to produce hot gases that rush out and shoot the rocket up into the air.

- Popcorn is also like a small rocket. The popcorn kernel consists of white fibres of starch inside a tough, yellowish hull. When the corn is heated, the small amount of water in the starch turns to steam, builds up pressure, and Pop! – the fluffy white starch bursts out of the hard hull and the popcorn goes flying. If you cook popcorn in a pan without a lid, you will see that this force can shoot the popcorn quite a distance into the air. This is fun to watch, but it makes quite a mess!

How do roots know to grow down and not up ?

Roots always grow down and stems always grow up for the same reason. They are both sensitive to the force of gravity.

It's a good thing a gardener does not have to worry about planting seeds in the ground the right way up, or the job would take a lot longer! If you do plant a seed upside down, the roots begin growing from the top of the seed and the stem comes out from the bottom. Soon, however, they both turn around: a root always grows towards gravity, and a stem grows away from it.

Can you confuse a plant? Start seedlings growing in some earth in a jar. Then turn the jar on its side or upside down after the shoots have grown a short distance from the soil.

Plants, like animals, can respond to such things as gravity, light, and water that are important for their survival. Although you cannot see them moving, plants slowly grow towards favourable conditions and away from unfavourable ones. The actual change in direction of growth is brought about by hormones in the plant.

If roots grow down in response to gravity, what would they do if there was no gravity? This experiment has actually been done. An orbiting spacecraft is free from the pull of Earth's gravity, and everything on board it becomes weightless. In an experiment suggested by schoolchildren, seeds were grown on a flight of the United States space shuttle. The result? The seeds grew roots which curled around and pointed in all directions, showing that they really need gravity to help them grow straight down.

Plant Journey

One of the most important responses of a growing plant is to move towards light. Plants use the energy of light to produce food in their leaves. In this *amazing* experiment, you can see just how persistent a growing shoot can be in its search for light!

Things you need
- 3 bean seeds
- cardboard box with dividers and lid
- small pot
- potting soil
- masking tape or Magic Plus tape

What to do
1. Plant the seeds in potting soil in the small pot, and water them.
2. Cut holes about 5 cm (2 in) across in the dividers of the box to make a maze, as shown in the illustration on the next page. Make one hole in the outside wall of the box.

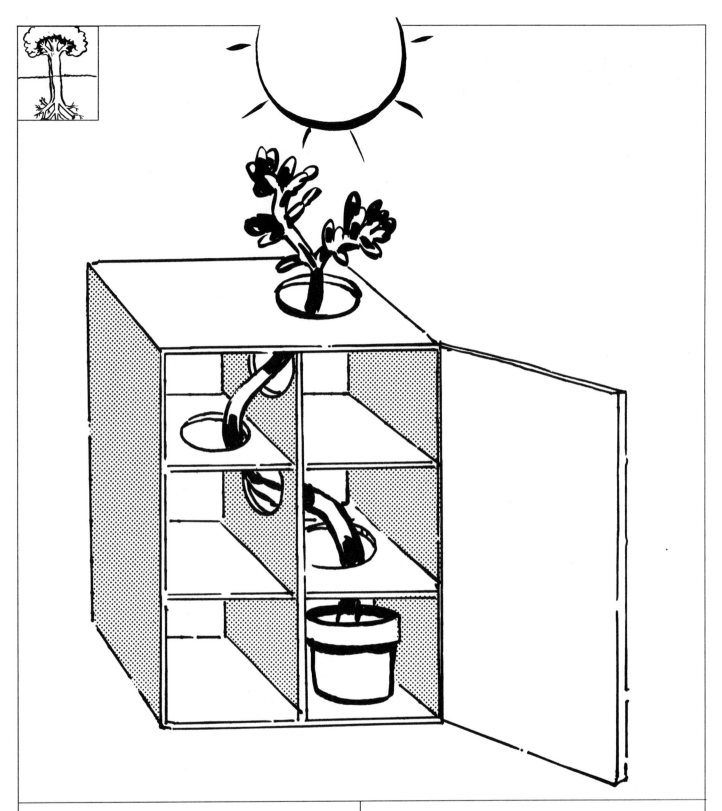

3. Place the pot of seeds in the box at the side opposite the hole in the outside wall. Close the lid and tape it so that no light can get through the lid.

4. Place the box with the outside hole facing a sunny window. Open the box every few days to water the seedlings, then reseal it. Eventually, the growing stems will find their way through the maze to the outside of the box.

Explanation
The shoots respond to the light by growing towards it.

DID YOU KNOW ???

- Some plant buds can measure temperature, telling the plant when it's warm enough to open its leaves.

- Climbing plants are sensitive to contact — they send out tendrils that move around until they touch a support and then grab onto it.

- The largest seed in the world is that of the coco-de-mer, which grows in the Seychelles Islands in the Indian Ocean. A single seed can weigh 18 kg (40 lb).
- The carrots that you eat are actually swollen roots. If a carrot hits an obstacle such as a stone as it is growing down through the soil, it will grow to one side, then continue downwards. That is why you sometimes see carrots with funny bends in them.

- The purpose of a root is to find water and to hold a plant in the soil.

- A growing root is so strong that it can crack a sidewalk and even force its way into hard granite.

Why does the Sun seem to follow you as you drive along in a car

The Sun seems to keep up with you in a moving car because of the way that your brain judges distances.

As you look out of the window of your car, nearby objects, such as telephone poles and trees beside the road, seem to move past very quickly. Things farther away, such as a farmhouse across a field or a tree some distance off, seem to move by a little more slowly. Very distant objects on the horizon can appear in the same position for a long time.

Because the Sun is over 150 000 000 km (93,000,000 mi) away from you and your

car, it seems to stay in the same place in relation to your car no matter how fast you travel. This gives the illusion that the Sun is moving along with you. The only thing that travels fast enough to make the Sun appear to move in the sky is the Earth itself, which rotates on its axis at a speed of 1670 km/h (1037 mph). Of course, you are also travelling along at this speed in space as you ride on the surface of planet Earth. When you see the Sun move below the horizon at sunset, it's a little like looking out of our planet's window at the passing scenery of space!

Cover-up

If you hold a coin at arm's length, you can cover the Moon with it – but that does not mean the Moon and the coin are the same size! In this experiment, you can see how your eyes work to judge distance.

Things you need
- cup
- coin
- friend

What to do
1. Place the cup on a table and stand about 3 m (9 ft) away.
2. Cover one eye and have your friend hold a coin at arm's length above the table.
3. Using only one eye to judge the position of the coin and the cup, direct your friend to move the coin until it is directly over the cup. Then have your friend drop the coin into the cup. How close did you come?

Explanation
The process you normally use to judge distances uses both eyes. Your two eyes see slightly different views of the world because they are set a short distance apart. Your brain compares the different images it gets from your two eyes and recreates a three-dimensional view. With practice, you can learn to judge distance through one eye by using other clues such as size and brightness.

DID YOU KNOW ???

- You can see the two different images you get from each eye if you look at something with only one eye, then with the other eye only, and rapidly switch back and forth a few times. This makes the object seem to jump around against the background, as you swap one view for another.
- Astronomers can calculate the distance to some nearby stars by using the different angles to the star measured from two opposite points in the Earth's orbit. Knowing the distance between these two points, and the angles, it is easy to calculate the distance to the star.
- Stereo sound works in the same way with your ears as stereo vision does with your eyes. Each ear gets a slightly different sound, and your brain merges the two sounds. Microphones placed at both sides of a concert hall or recording studio pick up slightly different sounds. The sounds recorded by one microphone are played back through one speaker on your stereo radio or headphones; the sounds recorded by the other microphone are played back through the other speaker. As you listen, you have the illusion of being there with the musicians!
- Animals turn their heads or ears to discover where a particular sound is coming from. By turning, they can compare the sounds that reach each of their ears. Try blindfolding a friend, make a noise a short distance away, and see if your friend can point to where you are without turning his or her head. Is it easier to find you if you make the sound in front of your friend or to the side?

If you have a baseline of a known length, and measure the angle from each end of the base to a distant object, the distance to the object can be worked out. This is the same thing your brain does to estimate distance. It compares the angles to an object seen from each of your eyes, which are a fixed distance apart.

Why does the sky look black in photographs of Earth taken by astronauts on the Moon ?

*T*o find out why the sky looks black from out in space, you must first understand what makes the sky look blue from the Earth.

The light that reaches Earth from the Sun actually consists of a mixture of different colours. You can see these colours when sunlight is split into a rainbow by raindrops or by a prism hanging in your window. The colours are always in the same order, with red at one end and blue at the other. Before it reaches the surface of the Earth, the sunlight must first pass through about 100 km (60 mi) of the Earth's atmosphere. There are countless tiny floating particles of fine dust in the atmosphere, and when the sunlight hits these, it bounces off them and scatters. The different colours scatter by different amounts, with blue and violet being scattered most. It is this scattering of the blue light by the atmosphere that makes the sky appear blue.

When you look at the Earth from the Moon, the sky looks black simply because the Moon has no atmosphere. There are no dust particles floating about to scatter the sunlight. The clear, airless surroundings of the Moon allow you to see into the blackness of space.

You cannot see unless there is something to reflect it. Try shining a flashlight or a car headlight on a very clear night. Then spray some mist or blow some talcum powder into the path of the light.

Sky in a Jar

Things you need
- clear jar or glass filled with water
- 1/4 cup of milk
- flashlight
- spoon
- square of black cardboard or black paper

What to do
1. Hold the black card behind the jar of water and shine the flashlight down through the water. Does the water have any colour? Can you see the black card through the water?
2. Stir a spoonful of milk into the water and look again at the water and the card. Continue adding milk a spoonful at a time. You should see at first a blue colour and then a pinkish colour in the water. The black card will become invisible.

Explanation
When you shone the light into clear water, you could see right through the water to the black card. This is like the view from the Moon into black space. When you added milk, you created an an "atmosphere," full of particles that scatter the light. The liquid appeared blue because the particles scattered the blue light. After you made your "atmosphere" thicker, the pink colour appeared, just as it does in the real atmosphere at dawn and dusk.

DID YOU KNOW ???

- Light travels in the form of waves, and each colour has a different wavelength. Blue and violet have short wavelengths; red and orange have longer wavelengths.

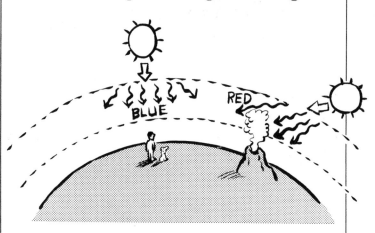

- The sky appears red at sunrise and sunset because the sunlight has to pass through more of the Earth's atmosphere when it is near the horizon than it does at noon when it is overhead. Because of this extra distance, some of the blue light gets scattered right out, and the red is what is left.
- Volcanic eruptions and forest fires give spectacular colours to the sky because they increase the amount of dust in the atmosphere.
- The sky on the planet Mars looks pink; on Titan, one of the satellites of the planet Saturn, it looks red. This is because of the different materials in their atmospheres.
- Stars appear to twinkle because of the effect of the Earth's atmosphere on the paths of light from the stars. Molecules of air and particles of dust are spread unevenly through the atmosphere and keep moving around. Light from a star passing through the atmosphere is bent first one way, then another, as it encounters these obstacles in its path. This makes it appear as if the star is constantly shifting its position slightly in the sky. The star seems to shimmer.

• When you watch a sunset, the Sun has actually gone below the horizon three or four minutes before it appears to. The sunrise is another illusion: you see the Sun appear a few minutes before it actually rises above the horizon. As light from the Sun enters the Earth's atmosphere, its path is bent, sending an image of the Sun above the horizon.

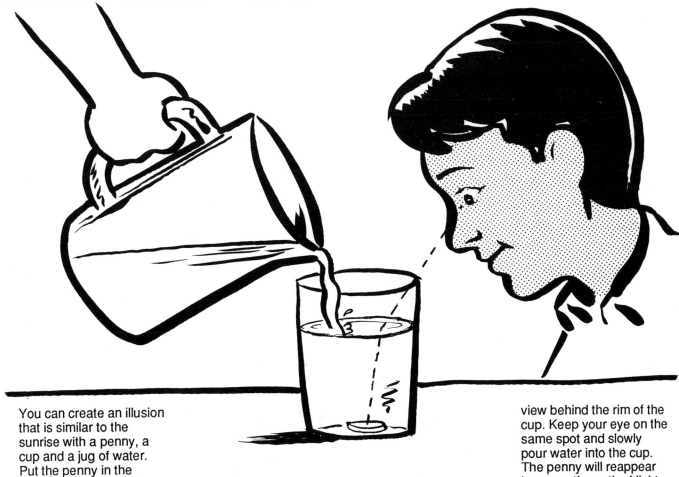

You can create an illusion that is similar to the sunrise with a penny, a cup and a jug of water. Put the penny in the bottom of the cup and move your head until the coin is just hidden from view behind the rim of the cup. Keep your eye on the same spot and slowly pour water into the cup. The penny will reappear because the path of light is bent as it passes from the water into the air.

When you fill a glass with water, how can the water rise above the rim of the glass

The reason this can happen is because molecules of water are strongly attracted to one another. The molecules on the surface of the water are pulled down towards those below them.

The attraction of water molecules to each other makes the surface of water act as if it had a thin skin over it. This effect is called surface tension. The force of the attraction is so great that it allows the water to rise a little above the walls of the glass, stretching this "skin" just like a rubber balloon.

How much can you make the water surface stretch? In the kitchen sink or other place where spills won't matter, fill a glass with water. Use a drinking straw to transfer water to the glass drop by drop. Even after the glass looks full to bursting, you can usually add more drops before it overflows. An alternative demonstration is to add pennies to the full glass of water. Slip them in gently from the side of the rim. You will be surprised at how many you can add before the water spills over.

The skin produced by surface tension is strong enough to allow some insects to literally walk on water. You may have seen some skipping across the surface of a pond. The weight of these insects is not enough to break the surface, and they can walk on water without even getting their feet wet!

You can even rest a metal paper clip on the water's surface. Take a dry paper clip and place it on a small piece of toilet tissue. Carefully place the paper with the clip on the water surface. Unfold another paper clip and use the end of it to gently push the tissue below the surface of the water. The paper clip will be left on the surface. It isn't floating. (If you want to know why, see the question about floating on page 32.) If you look closely at the surface of the water in a good light, you can actually see that the surface is bent under the clip, like a sheet of rubber.

Soap-powered Boat

The attraction of water molecules to each other can be weakened by adding soap. Try filling a glass as full as you can, then add a drop of liquid dishwashing detergent. This breaks the surface tension and the water spills. You can use this effect to make a boat powered by surface tension.

Things you need
- cardboard
- piece of soap or liquid soap
- bathtub, sink, or large bowl

What to do
1. Cut a small boat out of cardboard as shown.
2. Fill the bathtub, sink, or bowl with water.
3. Put a small piece of soap or liquid soap in the notch cut at the back of your boat.
4. Place your boat on the surface of the water and watch it go!

Explanation
The soap reduces the surface tension of the water around it. Since the surface tension is greater at the front of the boat than at the rear, it pulls the boat forward.

DID YOU KNOW ???

- Soap molecules attract water at one end and grease at the other. Water on its own is repelled by grease, but the addition of soap helps get grease off dishes.
- Surface tension explains why water flows smoothly from a tap. The water molecules on the outside pull towards those at the centre, holding the stream of water drops together in a column.

Make three small holes close together near the bottom of a can. Fill the can with water. If you pinch the three water streams together with your fingers, they will stay together as one stream – held there by surface tension.

- Dewdrops or rainwater stand in round drops on a leaf or petal surface rather than spreading out. This happens because the water molecules pull in towards the centre of the drop. The waxy surface of a leaf also repels the water.
- If you rub soap on a mirror in the bathroom, it will prevent the mirror from misting up. The soap does not allow the water vapour to condense into drops of water.
- Soap and water together make bubbles because the soap allows the water to stretch out more than usual. If you add glycerine to the mixture, your bubbles will last even longer because the glycerine slows down the evaporation of the water.

Try putting drops of different liquids such as milk, vinegar, oil, water, pop, and detergent on a sheet of smooth cardboard or paper and comparing their shapes. Those liquids which stand up in round globules have the strongest surface tension, and those which spread out flat have the weakest. The differences in their surface tension are due to the differences in the attraction of their molecules to one another.

Recipe for Making Monster Bubbles

Mix 3 cups of water with 2 cups of glycerine (you can get this at the drugstore) and 1 cup of *clear* dishwashing detergent.

Why does my voice sound different when I have a cold

The sound of your voice depends on the vibration of your vocal cords. Often when you have a sore throat your vocal cords become swollen. The vocal cords are found in the voice box (larynx) at the front of your throat. They work something like a reed instrument. Air from your lungs is pushed past the cords and sets them vibrating to produce sound. The pitch of your voice depends on the length and thickness of your vocal cords. The shorter and tighter they are, the higher the pitch.

The shape of your vocal cords is changed by muscles attached to them. Make a low humming noise, then try for as high-pitched a sound as you can manage. Notice that the higher pitch takes more effort – you are using muscles to stretch your vocal cords tighter.

Another thing that affects the sound of your voice is the size of your head or, more strictly, the spaces or sinuses inside it. The throat, mouth, nose, and nasal sinuses add resonance to the voice – like the hollow box of a guitar or violin. Children's sinuses are not well-developed, so their voices have a thinner, less rich quality than the voices of adults. This is another reason why your voice sounds different when you have a cold. Your sinuses and nose are blocked, and your voice sounds flatter, with less resonance.

The final thing that affects your voice is your tongue and lips, which make the precise sounds of different words by altering the shape of your mouth. When you have been to the dentist and had a "freezing" injection in your mouth, you may find it hard to speak normally until the anaesthetic wears off and you get back control of your mouth muscles. The same difficulty in speaking is found in stroke victims whose facial muscles have become paralysed.

The sounds that you make depend on the length of your vibrating cords and the size of your resonating spaces. You can hear the effects of both these things in two simple experiments.

A. A Simple String Instrument

Things you need
• cord, about 1.5 m (5 ft) long

What to do
1. Tie one end of the cord to the doorknob of a closed door. Stretch the cord tight and place your foot on the other end of the cord to hold it.

2. Pluck the cord with your finger, and listen to the sound it makes.
3. Grip the cord tightly between the thumb and forefinger of your other hand and see what effect that has on the sound of the string when you pluck it. Change the position of your grip up and down the cord as you pluck, and see if you can make a tune.

Explanation
Vibrating objects produce sounds by sending sound waves through the air. The pitch of the sound depends on the number of times that the object vibrates in a second. The greater the number of vibrations, the higher the sound. As you slide your hand along the string, you alter its length. A shorter length vibrates more frequently and so produces a higher sound.

B. Bottled Music

Things you need
- 4 or more identical bottles
- water
- pencil or pen

What to do
1. Pour a different amount of water into each bottle.
2. Line up the bottles and strike them with the pencil. You will get a different note from each. You can "tune" your bottles by changing the water levels to change the notes.
3. Now blow across the top of each bottle to produce a sound. The scale is reversed. Why?

Explanation
The first sounds are made by the vibrating glass. The water in the bottles slows these vibrations. The more water in the bottle, the slower the vibrations, and the lower the sound. The second sounds (made when you blow across the bottles) are produced by the air vibrating in the bottles. The less air, the faster it vibrates, and the higher the sound. In this case, therefore, the bottle with the most water — and the least air — has the highest sound!

DID YOU KNOW ???

- A man's voice is generally deeper than a woman's because a man's larynx is bigger – about 5 cm (2 in) long – and his vocal cords vibrate more slowly. At adolescence, a boy's voice "breaks." At this time, male sex hormones cause his larynx to increase growth and his voice deepens.

- When people get angry or emotional, their muscles tighten, and the pitch of their voice rises. The same thing happens if you become nervous, as when you have to make a speech in front of a group.

You can use a blade of grass to make a whistle that works like your vocal cords. Stretch the grass blade tightly between your thumbs and blow across it. You should obtain a whistle as the grass vibrates.

- There is no noise in space because there is no air. Sounds depend on the vibration of air molecules to produce sound waves.

- A songbird doesn't use its larynx for singing; it has a special sound-producing organ called a *syrinx*. This is a complex organ composed of cartilages and membranes, each of which the bird can control independently.

- A tape recording of your voice always sounds different from the way you normally hear your voice. That is because you usually hear your own voice in a different way! You hear the tape-recorded voice after the sound has travelled through the air. This is how you hear other people – and how they hear you. When you are speaking, however, part of your voice travels to your ear through vibrations in the bones of your skull.

- If you overwork the muscles of your vocal cords by talking, singing, or shouting too much, you may become hoarse. The muscles become too tired to do their job.

Why does long hair stick to a sweater when you pull the sweater over your head

The answer is static electricity. You can make two objects become electrically attracted to each other by rubbing them together and then drawing them apart – especially if the air is very dry. The rubbing scuffs off electrically charged particles from one of the objects and moves them to the other. The particles, called electrons, have a negative electrical charge. The object which *gains* electrons becomes *negatively* charged, while the object which *loses* electrons is left with a *positive* charge. Since opposite charges attract, the two objects are now attracted to one another.

If you run a plastic comb briskly through your hair on a dry day, it will pick up electrons and become negatively charged with static electricity. The comb will then attract small pieces of paper as if it were a magnet. If you hold the charged comb near a stream of running water, it will draw the water toward itself.

When you build up enough static electrical charge between two objects, electrons will actually leap across a gap from one to the other, like a miniature flash of lightning. That is what happens after you take your sweaters and nylon clothes from the tumble dryer. All that friction and heat builds up a strong charge, which makes the clothes cling to each other. When you pull them apart, electrons flying across the gap are seen as sparks.

KITCHEN DEMO

An Indian Thread Trick

Things you need

- balloon
- cotton thread, about 15 cm (6 in) long
- masking tape or Scotch tape

What to do
1. Tape one end of the piece of thread to a tabletop.
2. Inflate the balloon and rub it briskly against a rough sweater.
3. Hold the balloon above the piece of thread. The free end of the thread will leap up into the air towards the balloon. If you hold the balloon still, the thread will remain standing straight up as if by magic.

Explanation
The balloon becomes charged with static electricity when you rub it on your sweater. The electric charge attracts the thread and pulls it up toward the balloon.

Static electricity and thunderstorms

Have you ever got an electric shock from a doorknob on a cold, dry day? If you shuffle along a carpet and then reach out to a metal doorknob – Zap! Sparks fly from the knob to your fingertips and there is a sharp crackling sound. What happened is that you rubbed electrons off your body onto the carpet as you shuffled along. This left you with a positive charge that pulled loose electrons from the doorknob as soon as you came close enough.

The flash and crackle you got from the doorknob is a miniature version of lightning and thunder. On stormy days, static electricity builds up in clouds because of the friction between ice crystals and water droplets moving rapidly inside the clouds. The Earth acts like a huge doorknob, and electrons violently leap the gap between the clouds and the ground to produce lightning. The heat from the lightning rapidly warms the air, causing the air to expand. (For more about heat and expanding gases, see page 13.) The air contracts rapidly when it meets cooler air, and this vibration creates sound waves that you hear as thunder. (The question on page 27 explains how sound is produced.)

You can stick a balloon onto the ceiling with static electricity. Rub the balloon rapidly on a sweater to give it a charge. As you bring the balloon close to the ceiling, the negative charge on the balloon will repel the negative electrons on that part of the ceiling. This leaves an area with a positive charge, which attracts the balloon and holds it against the force of gravity!

- Static electricity tricks work better in dry air because water vapour molecules in the air knock excess electrons off charged objects and make them neutral again.
- TV pictures are formed by streams of electrons scanning a fluorescent screen. These electrons build up a static charge on your TV screen, which is why it sometimes crackles when you put your hand near it, and why it attracts dust.
- A lightning flash can be up to 32 km (20 mi) long. The energy from lightning can momentarily heat the air to 30 000°C (54,000°F) – more than five times hotter than the surface of the Sun!

- The word "electricity" comes from the Greek word *elektron*, which means "amber." Thales, a Greek philosopher (640-546 B.C.), discovered static electricity when he rubbed a piece of amber on his clothes and found that the amber then attracted small pieces of wood.
- Static electricity is what causes plastic food wrap to stick to itself and to food containers. Some of the charge is produced when the roll of plastic film is manufactured, but you can increase its cling by unrolling it fast as you pull off the piece you need.

Why is it easier to float in salt water than in fresh water ?

The answer to this lies in the fact that salt water is heavier than fresh water.

If you drop a small object into a glass of water, you will see that it pushes some of the water out of its way and makes the water level in the glass rise. The volume of water it pushes out of its way (displaces) is always the same as the volume of the object underwater.

If the weight of the water displaced by an object is also the same as the weight of the object, then the object will float. But if the weight of the water it displaces is less than the weight of the object, the object will sink. To put it another way: an object will float if it displaces a volume of water that weighs exactly the same as itself.

Salt water is denser than fresh water — that is, a cup of salt water weighs more than a cup of fresh water. A floating object will therefore displace a smaller volume of salt water than of fresh water, and the object will float higher on the surface of the salt water. For this reason, salt water can keep a heavier object afloat than fresh water can.

KITCHEN DEMO

The Magic Egg Trick

Will an egg float? Will it float in salt water? If fresh water is lighter than salt water, will fresh water float on salt water? This experiment answers all these questions!

Things you need
- egg
- glass
- water
- salt
- teaspoon

What to do
1. Carefully place the egg in a glass half full of water. It will sink.
2. Stir salt into the water, one teaspoonful at a time. The egg will gradually float up as you add more salt.
3. When the egg is floating at the surface of the salt water, carefully add more water to nearly fill the glass. Dribble it slowly over a spoon

held against the side of the glass, so that the fresh water doesn't mix with the salt water. You will end up with the egg floating on the boundary in between the fresh and salt water layers.

Explanation
The weight of fresh water displaced by the egg weighs less than the egg, so the egg will not float on fresh water. The weight of the salt water displaced by the egg, however, is the same as the weight of the egg, and the egg floats on the salt water. Fresh water will float on salt water as long as the two don't get mixed together.

DID YOU KNOW ???

- The weight of a particular volume of a substance is called its *density*. The density of water, for example, is one gram per cubic centimetre (62.4 lb/cu ft) Wood, cork, and polystyrene are less dense than water, and so they float. Stone, iron, lead, and gold are denser, and so they sink.
- Animals and plants are made up mostly of water, and so they will float just below the surface. Some fish, such as sharks, are denser than water. They must swim or they will sink to the bottom!

- Buoyancy, the ability to float, depends on volume as much as on weight. A tonne of lead sinks, but a tonne of wood floats. Both have the same weight, but a tonne of wood has a much bigger volume than a tonne of lead. It therefore displaces a much greater weight of water.
- The density of the planet Saturn is so low that the planet would float in water! Saturn, which is 744 times larger than Earth, is made up mostly of hydrogen gas.
- Warm water is less dense than cold water, and floats on top of it. When a warm ocean current meets a cold ocean current, the two do not mix: the warm water flows above the cold water.

How can a metal ship float? A hundred-thousand-tonne supertanker can float because its weight is spread out over a large volume. Most of the volume of a ship is, in fact, air space, with the metal wrapped around it. The density of the ship – metal and air together – is less than the density of the water it displaces.

33

Can You Make a "Water Parfait?"

cold salt water   cold fresh water   hot salt water   hot fresh water
(most dense)   (least dense)

1. Take four glasses. Put cold salt water in the first, cold fresh water in the second, hot salt water in the third, and hot fresh water in the fourth.

2. Add a different colour of food dye or ink to each glass (e.g., red, yellow, green, blue).

3. Take a tall glass and carefully pour the coloured water from each glass into it, beginning with the cold salt water and ending with the hot fresh water. Take care not to mix the layers.

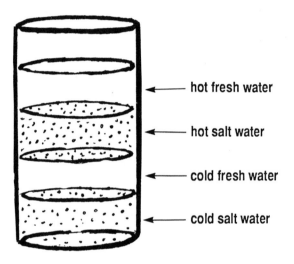

← hot fresh water

← hot salt water

← cold fresh water

← cold salt water

34

Why don't hens break their eggs when they sit on them ?

*I*t's all in the shape. Whether you want to crush, bend, twist, or slice an object, its shape is as important to its strength as what it's made of. Although an eggshell may be quite fragile, the shape of an egg gives it tremendous strength.

You can easily see the importance of shape if you build different bridges out of cardboard. For example, take two strips of cardboard, place one on top of the other, and lay them across the top of two equal piles of books. This bridge will barely support an empty jar. You can greatly strengthen the bridge, however, if you take the lower strip and bend it into an arch, with its two ends braced against the bottom of the book piles and its top pressing against the other strip of cardboard. This new structure will easily support a jar filled with sand or water.

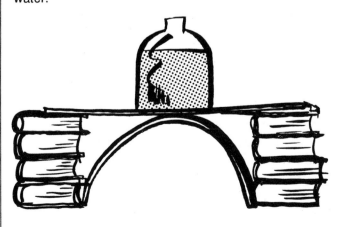

The arch is one of the strongest structures known for supporting a load. The dome, which is just a three-dimensional arch, is often used to cover extra large buildings, such as sports stadiums. The dome shape carries the weight of the roof evenly through its curved walls to the broad base, so that no single point on the dome supports the whole load. This shape has the advantage of not needing pillars to support the roof: pillars would get in the way of people's view.

Does the shape of the dome remind you of anything? An egg has the shape of two domes put together – which is why it's so strong.

Can you drop an egg two metres without breaking it?

Sure. Just hold it three metres above the ground and let it go. It will fall two metres without breaking. After that – watch out!

KITCHEN DEMO

Egg-straordinary!

Can you sit on an egg without breaking it? Find out in this experiment.

Things you need
- 4 eggs
- small pair of scissors
- masking tape
- several large books about the same size (e.g., encyclopedia volumes)
- weight scale

What to do
1. At the sink, gently break each egg at the narrow end by tapping it sharply with a spoon. Peel back a little of the broken shell and empty the contents.
2. Stick a piece of masking tape around the middle of each shell to prevent it from cracking when you cut it.
3. Carefully cut around each eggshell, through the masking tape, so that you end up with four half-shells of equal size, with level bottoms.

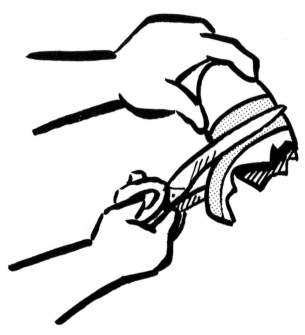

4. Place the eggshell domes on a smooth, clean floor or tabletop in a rectangle slightly smaller than your books.

5. Lay a book on the eggshells. Then another. Do the shells crack? Keep adding books. *Important:* In order for this experiment to work well, you must make sure the shells don't move when you add each book. If there is any twisting or pushing on the shells, they will break more easily. The weight must all be placed straight down on top of them.

6. Continue adding books until the shells crack. Weigh all the books to see how much weight the eggs could take. It should be much more than the weight of a chicken!

Explanation
The dome shape of each shell distributes all the weight evenly and minimizes stress and strain. Demonstrations at the Ontario Science Centre in Toronto have shown that a single hen's egg can support 90 kg (200lb)!

The strong arch form can still be seen in modern structures such as bridges made of steel or concrete.

- Arches are so strong that arches in buildings constructed by the Romans nearly 2000 years ago are still standing in good condition today.
- The largest hen's egg ever recorded weighed 453 g (1 lb) and had a double shell.

- Most of the hard part of an eggshell is made of calcium – the same material found in teeth and bones. Calcium dissolves in acid, so if you leave an egg in vinegar (which is an acid) for a few days, you will end up with a shell-less egg!

Why does pop fizz

The fizzing noise is made by the bursting of hundreds of tiny bubbles of carbon dioxide gas that form when the can or bottle of pop is opened. The spray is caused by the bursting bubbles pushing droplets of liquid up from the surface of the drink.

Soft drinks are carbonated. That is, carbon dioxide gas is dissolved in the liquid. The gas gives the drink its sparkle and tangy taste, and prevents it from spoiling. Carbonation is carried out by chilling the liquid and letting it flow over a series of plates in an enclosure that contains carbon dioxide under pressure. The lower the temperature and the higher the pressure, the more gas will dissolve in the drink.

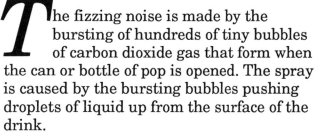

When you open the lid of a pop can or bottle, you release the pressure. The carbon dioxide comes out of solution to form the hundreds of tiny bubbles of gas that seem to appear from nowhere. (See the question about boiling water on a mountain, on page 10, for more information about gases and liquids).

If you shake a bottle of pop before opening it, what happens? The shaking causes some of the gas to come out of solution. This trapped gas builds up pressure in the bottle, and when you take the top off, the drink bursts out.

KITCHEN DEMO

Fizzzz

You can make your own super fizzy mixture by putting together two chemicals that make carbon dioxide gas.

Things you need
- 1/2 cup vinegar
- 3 tablespoons baking soda
- 1/4 cup water
- 5 drops liquid detergent (optional)
- 2-3 drops red food colouring (optional)
- tall glass, pan, or tray

What to do
1. Set the glass on the pan or tray and put the baking soda into the glass.
2. Add the liquid detergent and food colouring if you have them.
3. Add the water, and lightly stir the mixture.
4. Slowly pour the vinegar into the glass, and watch what happens.

Explanation

The baking soda and the vinegar combine in a chemical reaction that produces carbon dioxide gas. The gas bubbles up through the liquid, and the bubbles push the liquid up and out of the glass. The detergent produces extra bubbles, and the red colouring will create a dramatic effect!

DID YOU KNOW ???

- Some old fire extinguishers worked like a bottle of pop. They contained sodium bicarbonate solution and a container of sulphuric acid. When the extinguisher handle was turned, the container of acid was broken and the acid mixed with the sodium bicarbonate to produce carbon dioxide gas. The pressure of this gas forced the liquid out of the nozzle of the extinguisher in a forceful jet.
- If you sprinkle baking soda (sodium bicarbonate) on a grease fire, you get three fire extinguishers! The heat of the flames turns the sodium bicarbonate into three different chemicals: sodium carbonate, which is a white solid that smothers the flames; water, which cools the burning grease; and carbon dioxide, which smothers the flame by cutting off the supply of oxygen.
- The fact that baking soda produces carbon dioxide gas when heated is used in baking to make cakes lighter. The bubbles of gas rise up through the cake batter and make it light and spongy.
- In the United States, over 72 billion carbonated soft drinks are produced each year.

A Bubbling Centrepiece

Stir about three teaspoons of vinegar and two teaspoons of baking powder into a large jar of water until the liquid starts to fizz. Drop two or three mothballs, raisins, or peanuts into the jar and watch what happens. The objects will repeatedly rise and sink for some time. This is because the carbon dioxide gas bubbles formed by the reaction of the vinegar and baking powder cling to the objects and lift them to the surface. At the surface, the bubbles break, and the object sinks again. At the bottom, it starts to collect more bubbles, and the lifting process is repeated.

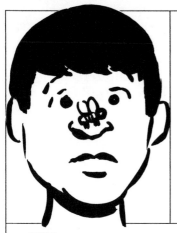

What makes you itch and how can you relieve the itching

*I*tching, or the feeling that makes you want to scratch, is caused by a mild stimulation of the nerve endings in your skin. Your skin is full of tiny sensors that react to changes in the environment around them. Some are sensitive to heat, some to cold, some to pressure, and others to pain. Each sensor lies at the end of a nerve. When the nerve ending is excited or stimulated by a sensor, small electric impulses travel along the nerve to the brain. The brain knows what the sensation is and where it came from, and sends out impulses for your body to take appropriate action – such as scratching!

The stimulation that gives you an itchy feeling can come from many sources. It might be a fly walking across your nose, or it might be caused by dry skin. A persistent itchy skin can also be a sign of liver or kidney disease. Sometimes, people get itchy because of allergies. An allergic reaction, for example to poison ivy, triggers the body to produce a chemical called *histamine*. This substance causes the skin to swell and get hot and produce rashes and an itching feeling. Anti-histamine drugs are sometimes used to control these allergic reactions and to relieve the itching feeling. Histamine is also found in the hairs of stinging nettles and in some insect venom, which is why insect or nettle stings make you itch.

KITCHEN DEMO

How Sensitive Are You?

Things you need
- pair of dividers (or unfolded paper clip)
- ruler
- friend

What to do
1. Have a friend sit down and close his or her eyes. Open the dividers so the points are about 5 cm (2 in) apart.
2. Touch the points of the dividers LIGHTLY on the back of your friend's hand. Make sure both points touch the skin at the same time, but do not press on the dividers! Ask your friend how many points he or she feels.
3. Remove the dividers, close up the space between the points slightly, and put them back on your friend's skin.
4. Continue to close the gap between the divider points until your friend reports feeling only one point instead of two distinct points. Write down the distance.
5. Repeat the experiment to find the skin's sensitivity to touch on the fingertip, upper arm, and cheek. Swap places with your friend and compare your results.

Explanation
Different parts of your body have different abilities to feel things touching the skin. Which part of your body was most sensitive? The smaller the gap between points that you can detect, the more sensitive the skin is in that part of your body. This experiment shows that there are more touch receptors in the skin at that area.

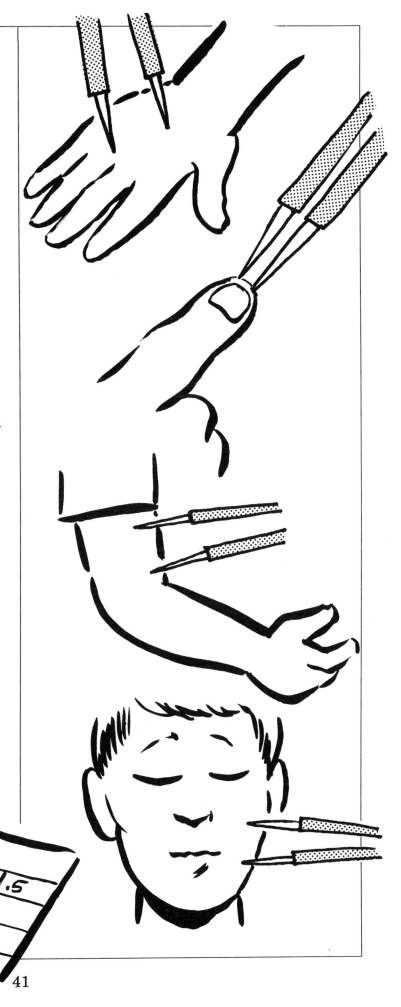

SITE	5	4	3	2	1	.5
BACK OF HAND						
FINGER TIP			X			
UPPER ARM						
TOES		X		X		
PALM						

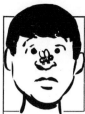

Try This

Touch the back of a friend's hair as gently as you possibly can, and have your friend say when he or she can first feel your touch. Does your friend feel the sensation of the touch before you do? Which part of your body is more sensitive to touch: fingertips or hair tips?

DID YOU KNOW ???

• About seventy percent of the population is allergic to poison ivy.

• You and everyone around you are continually shedding tiny bits of dead cells from the thin outer layer of skin. In fact, skin particles make up most of household dust. The entire outer layer of your skin is completely replaced by new growth every twenty-eight days!

- What is the largest organ in your body? Your skin! The skin of an adult weighs over 3 kg (6-7 lb). That is about twice the weight of the average human brain!

- A person's skin colour is determined by pigments in the outer layer of skin. One of these pigments, called *melanin*, protects the skin from the Sun's burning rays. The more pigment you have, the darker the colour of your skin.

- You have a lot more nerve ends in your hands and face than you do in your arms and legs.

Why does snow sometimes squeak when you walk on it

When snow is very cold, well below freezing, the snow crystals become dry and solid. When you walk on this snow, the solid crystals rub and grind against one another, making the squeaking noise you hear. When the temperature is just a little below freezing point (0°C, or 32°F), the pressure of your foot melts a little of the snow. This makes a thin layer of water beneath your foot, which lubricates the snow crystals so that they don't make a noise. It is only at very low temperatures that the ice cannot melt and you make the squeaky sound.

Ice Trick

See for yourself how ice is melted by pressure in this experiment.

Things you need
- water
- plastic or metal tray
- 60 cm (2 ft) length of wire, such as picture-hanging wire
- 2 large plastic jugs with lids
- plastic mixing bowl or food storage container

What to do
1. Make a large block of ice by freezing water in a suitable plastic container such as a mixing bowl or food storage container. The container does not have to be square in shape. It may take a day or two before the block is solid enough to use.

2. Fill two plastic jugs with water and put their lids on.
3. Tie the ends of the wire tightly around the handles of the two jugs.

4. Remove the ice block from the plastic container and stand it on a tray on the corner of a table. If it is winter, it is best to do this outside where the block will not melt so quickly.
5. Place the wire across the centre of the ice block and carefully let the jugs hang down on either side.
6. Allow the jugs to hang for several hours and check on them occasionally. You will see that the wire cuts into the ice, and becomes embedded in the block.

Explanation
The weight of the jugs of water makes the wire press tightly against the ice block, and the pressure alone causes the ice to melt underneath the wire. The wire moves down into the water, and the water freezes above it.

WATER

SNOW

- Ice skaters actually skate on water. The pressure of the skate blades causes the ice to melt and forms a slippery surface beneath the blades. It is difficult to skate when the ice is very cold, because the pressure of the blades is not great enough to melt the ice.
- Skiers also move on a film of water, but the melting of the snow is caused by friction, not pressure. Ebonite or wooden skis are better than metal skis because they do not conduct heat as well as metal. A good conductor allows the heat of friction to be lost quickly into the air, and does not maintain a water layer as well as a poor conductor does. If the weather is too cold, friction will not melt the snow. You must then wax the skis. This reduces the friction and allows you to ski over the harder surface.

- An avalanche is caused when a sudden warming melts some snow on a slope. The water formed by the melted snow acts as a lubricant and lets the remaining snow slide rapidly down the slope.
- When you make a snowball, the pressure on the snow as you squeeze it in your fist melts the surface of the snow. The water then refreezes and holds the ball together in a thin layer of ice.

Is science used in magic ?

*M*uch magic is based on surprise. You expect one thing, but something else happens instead. Both magic and science are based on people's belief that a particular act will result in a particular effect. Some magic uses science to achieve surprising effects.

Suppose you see a magician pour a clear liquid that looks like water into a glass containing another clear liquid. Suppose the resulting mixture turns bright red. It looks like magic. You don't usually get this result in everyday life when you mix two clear liquids together. If you are a chemist, however, you know that some colourless liquids can react together to produce a coloured chemical. If you know what the first two liquids are, the result is no surprise at all!

KITCHEN DEMO

These two tricks are based on the fact that metals gain and lose heat much more quickly than most other materials.

A. The Cloth That Will Not Burn

In this bit of scientific magic, you can make it appear that a handkerchief won't burn.

Things you need
- quarter
- old cotton handkerchief or other piece of cotton cloth
- pencil
- candle
- matches

✚ **SAFETY FIRST!** Make sure you keep the lit candle well away from objects that can burn.

What to do
1. Place the quarter in the centre of the handkerchief, and twist the cloth so that it is stretched tightly around the coin.

2. Light the candle.
3. Break the lead tip from a pencil and hold the wood in the candle flame until the wood glows red hot. Don't let the wood catch fire!

4. Press the red hot wood tightly against the handkerchief where it covers the coin, and hold it there for a few seconds.

5. Put the pencil down, unwrap the handkerchief from the coin, and shake the handkerchief out. Amazingly, there is no scorch mark on the cloth!

Explanation
Heat travels very quickly through metal. When the hot wood touches the handkerchief, the heat is conducted rapidly through the cloth into the metal coin. The heat does not stay long enough in the cloth to burn it.

B. Hot Money

Amaze your friends by picking out the penny they have chosen!

Things you need
- 6 one-cent coins, each with a different date
- plate
- bowl
- audience of friends or family

What to do
1. Before you begin this trick, slightly chill the pennies in a refrigerator.
2. Place all the pennies on a plate, and tell your audience that each coin has a different date. Ask someone to pick out one of the coins and pass it around the group so that everyone (except you) can see it and check the date.
3. When the plate of coins is returned to you, put all the coins into a bowl and shake them slightly to mix them up. Reach in without looking and pull out the coin that feels warmer than the others. Read out the date on the coin. You will have picked out the coin your audience chose!

Explanation
The warm hands of your audience rapidly heats the coin. You can pick out the warm coin from the others when you feel around in the bowl.

- Harry Houdini was a famous magician who amazed audiences in the early part of this century with his ability to escape from ropes, handcuffs, and locked containers. Many of his spectacular escapes were made possible by his knowledge of locks and knots, and his ability to control his muscles and contort his body.

Some magic tricks are based on an optical illusion.
1. Cut out a cardboard circle about 5 cm (2 in) across
2. Draw a bird on one side of the disk.

3. Draw a cage on the other side of the disk, making sure it is upside down in relation to the bird.

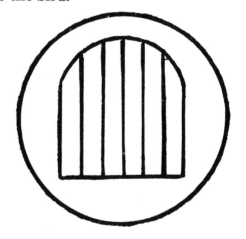

4. Punch two small holes near the edges of the disk and thread a string through them.

5. Twirl the disk and look at the pictures. There will appear to be only one picture — of a bird in a cage. This is because your eye holds each image for a short period of time. When you see two images in rapid succession, your brain joins them together into a single picture.

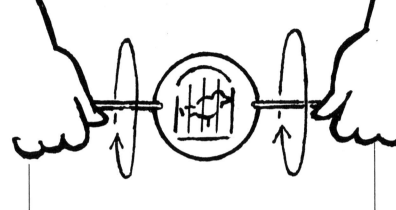

• Some magic tricks are based on numbers. This one will mystify your friends because it seems quite complex. When you examine the trick, however, you will see that the important calculation is very simple. The other calculations are put in to confuse and misdirect your audience — a common part of magic tricks.

Tell your audience to think of a number, then triple it, add 18, divide by three, and subtract the original number. Tell them the answer is 6. It will always be 6, no matter what number they first think of. The important calculation is dividing the 18 by 3 to give 6. All the other calculations cancel each other out and bring the number first thought of down to zero. Once you understand how this works, you can invent your own variation of the trick and make it as complex as you like.

How do sponges work

Sponges soak up water by a process called capillary action. This term describes the tendency of water to be pulled into very narrow tubes (called capillary tubes). You can see capillary action if you put the tip of a long, thin glass dropper into a glass of water. Some of the water will rise up into the tube. A sponge is full of a large number of narrow spaces and passageways that act like thin tubes. The thinner the tube, the farther the capillary action will draw the water along it.

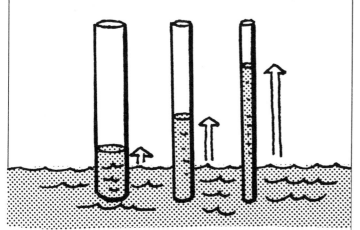

Capillary action is based on the attraction of molecules to one another. This is the same attraction that causes surface tension. (See the question about filling a glass with water above the rim on page 24). If you look at a glass of water, you will see that the water level is a little higher at the edge of the glass than it is in the middle. The glass pulls the water a little way up. If you dip one end of a strip of paper towel into a glass of water, you can see the water gradually rise up the paper. The water rises up by capillary action through the long narrow gaps between the fibres that make up the paper. This is exactly the same way that the sponge works. Capillary action is particularly important to plants. Fine tubes running up through the roots, stems, and leaves of plants help to draw water up from the ground to the top of even the highest trees by the process of capillary action.

KITCHEN DEMO

Coloured Celery

You can see how capillary action works in plants in this colourful demonstration.

Things you need
- glass of water
- stick of celery with some leaves on it
- food colouring

What to do
1. Half fill the glass with water and add a few drops of food colouring to it.
2. Cut a piece off the bottom of the celery stalk and place the stalk in the glass of coloured water.
3. Leave the celery in the glass for several hours and check on its appearance occasionally. You will see the colour gradually move up the stalk into the leaves.

4. After the colour has reached the tips of the leaves, remove the celery and cut across the stalk. You will see a row of tiny coloured circles.

Explanation
The coloured water is taken up the stem and into the leaves by capillary action through tiny tubes that run throughout the plant. The coloured circles you see in the stem are the ends of these small tubes, called tubules.

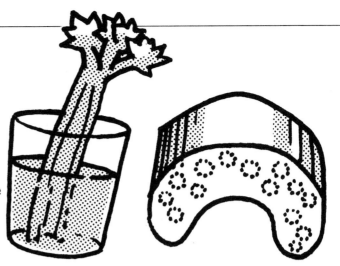

- Paint brushes use capillary action. The gaps between the bristles of the brush help draw the paint up the brush and hold it there until it is applied to the object being painted.
- A candle wick draws melted wax up to the flame by capillary action.

- You can see capillary action in your breakfast cereal. Big fibrous types of cereal soak up the milk by capillary action. If you are eating the small circular types of cereal, you may notice that they pull and cling together on the surface of the milk. They are held together by surface tension.

53

- A large tree might draw up 900 L (200 gal) of water through its tubules on a hot day. That's enough to fill your bathtub four times.

- Cultivated ground that is regularly ploughed or dug up keeps its moisture better than ground that is left to settle. That is because the digging opens up larger spaces in the soil and prevents water in the soil from rising by capillary action to reach the surface and evaporate.

- If you sit on damp ground, the moisture makes its way through your clothes by capillary action and you soon feel the damp against your skin. How quickly you feel the damp, however, depends on the material you are wearing. The open fibres of cotton cloth draw water up quickly. Polyester fabrics have more solid fibres with few spaces between them, and so water doesn't penetrate them very quickly.

54

Where do navel oranges and seedless grapes come from if they don't have seeds ?

Seedless plants are grown from bits taken from the parent plant's stem or leaves. A stem or leaf cutting put in water will grow roots and become a complete plant, identical to the plant from which the cutting was taken.

Making new organisms in this way is called *cloning*. It is a way of producing offspring from only one parent.

By growing new plants without seed, plant growers have more control over the process. They can also ensure that the characteristics of a good plant are all passed on to the offspring, because the offspring are literally part of the parent plant and are all identical to it.

New plants can also be grown without seed through a process called grafting. A plant that isn't fertile, or one that cannot produce good quality seeds, can be reproduced by inserting a young shoot into the roots or stem of another plant – even a plant of a different species. Many kinds of fruit trees are grown in this way.

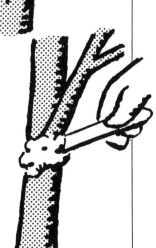

All of the small spider plants hanging from the parent plant are clones. They can be cut off and planted to make new plants identical to the parent.

Plant seeds are produced by sexual reproduction. This requires two parent plants – one to provide pollen and one to provide the egg, or *ovum*. The ovum develops seeds after it is fertilized by the pollen. Pollen is often carried from one flower to another by an insect, such as a bee. The offspring produced in this way have some of the characteristics of one parent and some of the characteristics of the other parent.

Two Plants from One

You can easily clone a plant at home.

Things you need
- plant, such as African violet
- potting soil
- water
- clay pot

What to do

1. Break a healthy leaf from the plant and place the stem of the leaf in water.

2. After a few days, you will see roots growing from the end of the stem. Plant the stem in some good quality potting soil in a clay pot, making sure you pack the soil firmly around the stem.

3. Place the cutting in a light, warm place, out of direct sunlight. Make sure the soil is always kept damp. Eventually, your cutting will sprout some new leaves and you will have another plant.

 DID YOU KNOW ???

- Scientists can now produce artificial seeds. The seed consists of the plant embryo, packaged in a plastic shell that will break down when the seed is planted. Plant fertilizers and pesticides can be included inside the package to give the artificial seed an advantage over natural seeds.

How are clouds formed ?

louds are made of water that has evaporated from the ground. Water rises into the sky as invisible water vapour. As it cools, it turns back into visible water droplets which cluster together to make up a cloud.

When the Sun shines on a river, lake, ocean, or puddle, the Sun's energy turns some of the water into a gas, — water vapour. This water vapour becomes a part of the air and travels around with the winds. Sometimes the vapour is carried up-wards, where two things happen to it. Its temperature goes down and so does the pressure of the air. These are the conditions that form clouds.

Cold air cannot hold as much water vapour as warm air. In the cooler air, the vapour condenses into liquid water, which we can see. In a cloud, the liquid drops start out very small and light, which easily float in the winds, like bubbles. When drops run into each other, they sometimes join to form bigger drops. If enough big drops form, they

will fall to the ground as rain. The rain ends up in rivers, lakes, and oceans, where the whole cycle can start over again.

A Cloud in a Bottle

Things you need
- large clear *plastic* soft drink bottle (torpedo-shaped)
- match
- warm water

✛ SAFETY FIRST! Try this experiment in a sink first. Matches can start fires!

What to do
1. Pour enough of the warm water into the bottle to just cover the bottom.
2. Light the match, blow it out, and then quickly hold the smoking match near the mouth of the bottle. Hold the bottle horizontally as you do this. Slowly squeeze the bottle, then release your pressure on it so a little smoke is drawn inside.

3. Put the top on the bottle, tighten it, and shake the water around to wash any condensation off the sides.

4. While holding the bottle up to a bright light, squeeze and release the bottle several times. Look closely in the centre of the bottle. You should see a cloud form every time the bottle is released, then disappear when the bottle is squeezed.

Explanation

Water vapour condenses when the air pressure is lowered. When you lower the pressure inside the bottle by releasing it, the water vapour from the hot water condenses. The interesting thing is that it doesn't happen without the smoke from the match. Water vapour forms liquid drops only around a tiny nucleus, such as a particle of dust or smoke.

DID YOU KNOW ???

- Clouds do not form only in the sky. Whenever warm moist air meets colder air, clouds will form. Your breath makes miniature clouds on a cold day, when the warm, moist air you breathe out cools and becomes visible in front of your face.

- The hot moist air coming out of a car exhaust pipe on a cold day condenses into a little cloud that follows the car around. When the car has been running for a while, the exhaust system gets hot enough to dry up all the water before it can reach the cold air outside the car, and the cloud disappears.

- If you live by the ocean, you know about fog, which is really just a cloud that cannot fly. Fog droplets are like those found in clouds, but they hover near the Earth's surface because of the lack of wind.

- Do your glasses "fog up" when you come inside on a cold day? The cold glass or plastic lenses cool the water vapour in the room and the water vapour condenses into a liquid on your glasses.

- Each water droplet in the atmosphere forms around a tiny nucleus, usually a particle of dust. Sometimes, water drops form around microbes floating in the air. In this case, when it rains, it's raining life!

How does the eraser on a pencil work

*E*rasers, like bicycle brakes, use friction to do their job. When you rub two surfaces together, friction is the force that resists the motion of one surface over the other. If the surfaces are perfectly smooth, there is very little friction, and the surfaces slide easily over one another. If the surfaces are rough, like sandpaper, the friction is much greater, and the surfaces are hard to rub together.

When an eraser is rubbed across paper, the friction between the eraser and the paper actually rubs off the top layer of the paper, taking the pencil mark with it.

KITCHEN DEMO

The Floating Bowl

Things you need
- glass bowl or dish with a smooth rim
- sink full of hot soapy water
- smooth counter surface

What to do
1. With the bowl and the counter dry, place the bowl upside down and try pushing it around on the counter surface.

2. Put the dish into the hot soapy water so it is completely submerged and leave it for a few minutes.
3. Using a dishcloth or a sponge, wet the surface of the counter with some of the soapy water.

4. Take the wet bowl out of the water and place it upside down on the counter. Carefully, without breaking the bowl, try sliding it again.

   Is there any difference in the way the bowl moves?

Explanation

When the bowl and counter are dry, the friction between the two makes it hard to move the bowl. The soapy water acts as a lubricant between the two surfaces and reduces the friction. At the same time, the hot air inside the bowl expands and escapes around the rim of the bowl, actually lifting the bowl slightly off the surface. This air layer reduces the friction even further.

If you leave the bowl to cool on the counter, it will become even more difficult to move it. When the cooling air inside contracts, it creates a suction that pulls the bowl onto the counter.

- Without friction, you could not walk or run. You use the friction between your shoes and the ground to walk. If there was no friction, your feet would slip out from under you.

- Tires use friction to grip the road. Without it, the wheels would just spin. Ice is such a smooth, low-friction surface that cars cannot easily start moving on it. Similarly, a car moving on ice cannot easily steer or stop because of the lack of friction.
- Although friction is needed to get things moving, it also gets in the way of moving. All the moving parts of a vehicle that rub against each other cause friction. The tires on the road and the air rubbing against the body of the vehicle also act to slow it down. A car travelling along the highway at 100 km/h (60 mph) spends almost half its energy overcoming friction.

- Astronauts floating weightless in space have no friction to slow them down, until they bump into something.
- When spacecraft return from orbit, they heat up because of the friction between them and the air as they plunge through the Earth's atmosphere.
- The heat created by friction in the atmosphere is also what causes fiery meteors, or shooting stars. These are solid objects from space that fall towards Earth. The heat of friction is so great that most of them are vapourized into a gas before they can make it to the ground.

- Bicycle brakes use friction between the rubber pads and the rim of the wheel to slow the wheel down. The harder you squeeze the brakes, the greater the friction and the faster you will stop. If you feel the rubber pads of bicycle brakes after making a hard stop, the pads will feel warm because of the heat produced by the friction.

ICE

What's the best way to get a car unstuck in snow?

Before you call for help, don't let the wheels spin.

A spinning wheel generates heat from friction. This melts the snow, but when the wheel stops, the water freezes into ice. This causes the wheel to spin even more. Eventually, you will dig a hole with the spinning and melting. If you put the car in low gear, the wheel turns more slowly, and you are more likely to get traction on the snow crystals.

WARNING: If you are the person pushing a stuck car on a cold day, don't put your face on the car's metal surface, or you could end up in pain. Moisture from your breath and on your lips can freeze when it touches cold metal and will stick your skin to the metal with a layer of ice. People often don't realize this has happened until they stand up, leaving a layer of skin behind on the car.

How do rainbows form?

Rainbows are created by a process called refraction. Refraction is the bending of light when it passes through one substance, such as glass or water, into another, such as air.

Light from the Sun is made of many different colours, and each colour bends by a different amount. When light from the Sun passes through a waterdrop floating in the air, it is refracted. All the different colours in the light are separated and become visible to the eye. The colours in a rainbow are always in the same order. The position of each colour depends on the amount by which it is bent.

KITCHEN DEMO

A Rainbow in a Glass

Things you need
- tall, clear glass of water
- flashlight

What to do
1. Hold the flashlight beside the glass so that the beam is shining through the middle of the water.
2. Hold a piece of white paper beside the flashlight, and look for a rainbow on the paper. You may have to adjust the position of the paper to find it.

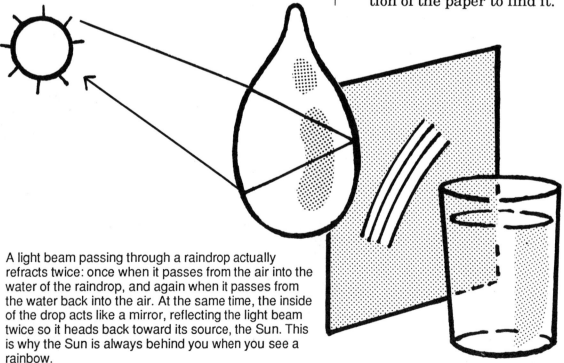

A light beam passing through a raindrop actually refracts twice: once when it passes from the air into the water of the raindrop, and again when it passes from the water back into the air. At the same time, the inside of the drop acts like a mirror, reflecting the light beam twice so it heads back toward its source, the Sun. This is why the Sun is always behind you when you see a rainbow.

Explanation

The glass of water acts like one large drop of water, bending the light and spreading out the colours. The rainbow that appears in front of the glass, spreading back toward the light source, is light that has been refracted and reflected twice, just like a rainbow. Another rainbow can be found behind the glass, made up of light that was refracted, but not reflected – light that passed right through the glass of water. It is this kind of refraction that can cause a rainbow around a light source, such as a ring around the Moon.

DID YOU KNOW ???

- Sundogs, miniature rainbows sometimes seen on either side of the Sun, are caused by ice crystals that just happen to have the right shape and be in the right position in the sky to create a rainbow. The crystals are shaped like tiny pencils, with their long sides pointing up and down.

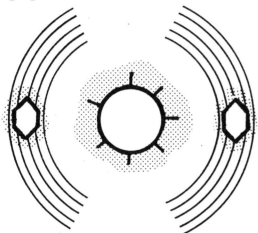

- Not all rainbows have colour. When waterdrops are extremely small, the spreading of light is not enough to separate the colours. As a result, the rainbow appears white.

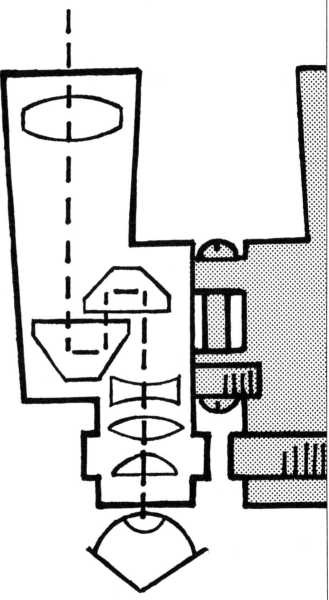

Refraction is used in binoculars to bend light around corners. The prisms in a pair of binoculars bend the light from the big lenses at the front closer together, so that you can see a wide field of view with your eyes.

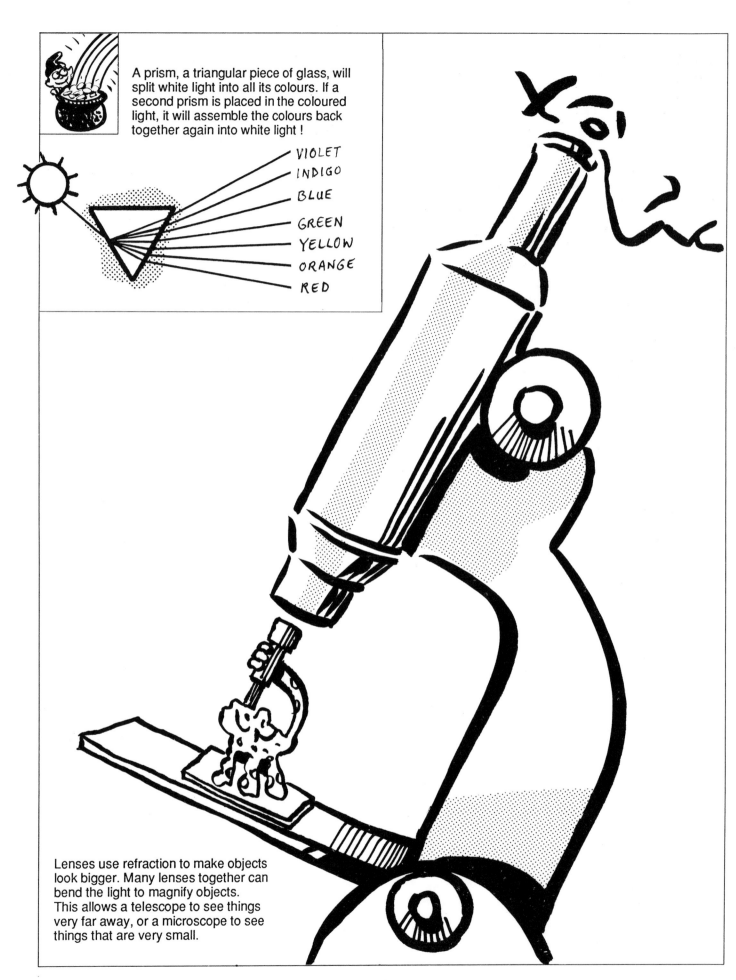

A prism, a triangular piece of glass, will split white light into all its colours. If a second prism is placed in the coloured light, it will assemble the colours back together again into white light !

VIOLET
INDIGO
BLUE
GREEN
YELLOW
ORANGE
RED

Lenses use refraction to make objects look bigger. Many lenses together can bend the light to magnify objects. This allows a telescope to see things very far away, or a microscope to see things that are very small.

Why do windows feel cold even though it is hot in the room

Windows feel cold because they do not absorb sunlight. When sunlight is absorbed by an object such as a desk or your body, the light energy is turned into heat energy. When light passes through something such as glass, it is not absorbed and therefore not turned into heat.

The interesting thing about windows is that they allow light to pass through but they stop heat. When sunlight shines into a room through a window, the light is absorbed by the objects in the room. The objects give off heat, which tries to escape back out through the windows. Because heat cannot pass through the glass, it remains trapped, and the room heats up by solar energy.

This is called the *greenhouse effect,* because it is used in greenhouses to keep plants warm, even in winter.

How to Make a Greenhouse

Things you need
- large clear glass bowl
- thermometer
- bright light, or a sunny day

What to do
1. Measure the temperature of the air by leaving the thermometer in the room (or outside in the shade) for a few minutes. Record the temperature on a piece of paper.
2. Place the same thermometer on a desk (or on the ground in the sun) and place the glass bowl upside down over top of it.
3. Allow sunlight to shine directly on the bowl, or shine a bright light directly over the bowl for five or ten minutes.
4. Read the temperature on the thermometer and compare it with the temperature of the air. Is there any difference ?

If you do this experiment outside on the grass, what else do you notice happening to the glass after it has been outside for a while?

Explanation
The glass allows the light to shine through and be absorbed by the desk top or the ground. The heat given back is trapped under the glass and raises the temperature of the air inside the bowl.

In the grass, condensation forms on the bowl because moisture given off by the grass is also trapped. When water vapour touches the cool glass, it condenses into drops.

- Carbon dioxide gas behaves in the same way as the glass in a greenhouse window by trapping heat. The planet Venus has an atmosphere made almost entirely of carbon dioxide, and has trapped so much heat that the surface of Venus is a scorching 600°C (1,112°F)
- Some scientists are worried that the burning of fossil fuels such as coal and oil is adding more carbon dioxide to the atmosphere of the Earth. This could cause a greenhouse effect and raise temperatures around the world. It may seem like a nice idea to live on a warmer planet, especially if you don't like winter, but too much warming could melt the polar ice caps and raise the level of the oceans so much that coastal cities would be flooded.

- Thermometers have to be kept in the shade to give an accurate temperature reading. In direct sunlight, the glass of the thermometer itself will trap heat and give a reading that is higher than the air temperature.

- Solar panels are painted black because black absorbs more light than any other colour. They are covered in glass to trap the heat given off by the black surface.

- You should be careful not to leave your pet in a closed car on a hot summer day. The car windows act like glass in a greenhouse, raising the temperature inside the car to the point where the pet will suffer or even die from heat exhaustion.

- Leaving car windows closed on a hot day can generate temperatures that will melt phonograph records or tapes left on the dashboard or seat.

Which freezes faster, warm water or cold water

This question took Wonderstruck a lot of research and experimenting to find the answer. According to theory, hot water should freeze faster because it evaporates faster, it loses its heat faster, and it also loses some of its volume as it cools. But when we tried it in our freezer, the cold water froze first every time.

When we asked some experts, some said that the cold water will freeze first because the warm water cannot freeze until it becomes what the cold water already is – cold. But others said that the hot water should freeze first because it cools at a faster rate.

It seems that hot water freezes faster only when it's outside, where the evaporating water is carried away by the wind. This leaves a smaller volume of water behind to freeze, which takes less energy. Therefore it should reach the freezing point in less time. In a refrigerator freezer, the vapour from the hot water is trapped. It condenses and falls back as water. The volume of hot water is not reduced, and as a result, it takes at least as long to freeze as the cold water.

If you try this simple experiment, make sure that you use two containers that are exactly the same shape, and that you use exactly the same amount of water in each.

KITCHEN DEMO

Hot or Cold?

Things you need
- 5 identical glasses
- a kettle
- salt
- water
- olive oil
- rubber gloves
- 2 metal teaspoons

✚SAFETY FIRST! Remember! Boiling water burns! To avoid breaking the glasses, put a metal teaspoon in each glass before pouring in the boiling water. Then remove the teaspoons.

What to do
1. Boil some water in the kettle and let it boil for about five minutes.
2. Carefully pour equal amounts of the boiling water into two of the glasses. Allow the water to cool.
3. Pour equal amounts of cold tap water into the other two glasses, and some olive oil into the last glass. All five glasses should now have equal amounts of liquid in them.
4. Put a teaspoon of salt into one of the glasses of cold tap water and stir.
5. When the boiling water has cooled enough, cover the top of one of the glasses with a rubber glove and shake it until the water fills with bubbles.
6. When all five glasses are at room temperature, place them in the freezer.

You could label them or make a note of their position in the freezer so that you know what is in each glass.
7. Check the glasses every quarter of an hour and record the order in which they freeze.

Explanation
The temperature at which water freezes is affected by several things. Impurities in the water raise the freezing temperature, so the glass with the tap water (which contains many impurities) should freeze first. Air is also an impurity in water, so the glass of boiled water that you shook bubbles into should freeze next. By boiling the water in the first place, you removed most of the dissolved air and some of the impurities. The glass of boiled water without the air bubbles is fairly pure, and therefore should freeze third. Very pure water can actually be cooled to -40°C (-40°F) without freezing. The glass with the salt should be the next to freeze, because salt lowers the freezing point of water.

The olive oil shows you another strange property of freezing water. Most liquids shrink when they freeze. The frozen olive oil takes up less space in the glass than the frozen water, although all five glasses started out with the same volume of liquid. Water is a very unusual liquid because it actually expands when it freezes. Water also freezes from the top down, while olive oil freezes from the bottom up. If you place the glasses on a counter and watch the liquids melt, you will see that the water melts from the bottom, while the olive oil (and most liquids) melt from the top.

- Water is one of the few liquids that expands when it freezes. As the water freezes, the molecules rearrange themselves into a crystal shape that is less dense than liquid water. That is also the reason ice floats. It's a good thing that ice floats, because if water contracted when it froze, like most other liquids, lakes would freeze from the bottom up, which would not be very healthy for the fish in the lakes.

- Glass is not really a solid, and it is not a frozen liquid. Glass is actually a very thick liquid that flows so slowly it retains its shape for many years. Old windows are actually thicker at the bottom than they are at the top because the glass has gradually flowed down like very thick molasses.

Why does water form a funnel shape when it goes down the drain

*T*he funnel of water swirling down a drain is called a *vortex*. This shape can be seen throughout nature in water and in air, and even in distant galaxies. Whatever its size, a vortex has a very stable shape.

The direction of spin in a vortex of water going down a drain is not related to the turning of the Earth as some people think. It depends more on the shape of the sink or tub, and on currents in the water. Observations in the Southern Hemisphere have shown that the drain water spins there in both directions, just as it does here.

Only very large vortices, like hurricanes, are affected by the turning of the Earth. They turn counterclockwise in the Northern Hemisphere and clockwise in the Southern Hemisphere.

A vortex can form when a fast-moving fluid meets a slow one, or when fluids moving in different directions meet, or when fluids of two different densities meet.

A. Drain Survey

Things you need
- as many sinks and bathtubs full of water as you can find in your home, or in those of your friends.

What to do
1. Fill a sink or bathtub with water, pull the plug, and notice whether the water swirls clockwise or counterclockwise down the drain.
2. Once the vortex forms, try stirring the water to make it spin in the other direction. Does it keep going in the opposite direction?
3. Repeat this for sinks and tubs of different shapes and sizes. Make a list of all the sinks and tubs, and the way the water spins in each. Do they all spin in the same direction?

B. Tornado In A Glass

Things you need
- two tall clear glasses filled with warm water
- food colouring (any colour)
- spoon

What to do
1. Put one of the glasses of water aside and let it sit for a few minutes undisturbed.
2. With the spoon, slowly stir the water in the second glass. Do not stir too quickly; there should only be a small "dimple" in the water at the surface.
3. Remove the spoon and place one drop of food colouring into the centre of the water surface. Watch the shape the food colouring takes. Try this again after stirring the water at different speeds and watch what happens.
4. When the water in the other glass is perfectly calm, carefully let one drop of food colouring fall onto the centre of the water surface. Look for a ring shape that gets wider as it falls through the water. You may also see smaller rings forming off the larger one.

Explanation
When the food colour hits the spinning water, it tries to sink to the bottom of the glass. This is because the food colouring is denser than the warm water. As it descends, it is spun into a vortex shape by the rotating water. If you look closely, you can sometimes see several layers in the funnel. The bigger the glass, the more dramatic the funnel will be.

The drop of food colour falling on the calm surface forms another kind of vortex called a *torroidal vortex*. When the drop hits the water, the edges of the drop are slowed down. The centre, moving faster, swirls around the edges, forming the ring shape. Smoke rings are torroidal vortices in air. If you try these effects with cold water instead of warm, they don't work as well. Why not?

- The flapping of a flag is caused by vortices of air coming off the pole. Air spinning off the sides of the pole alternates from one side to the other. As the vortices travel downwind away from the pole, they bend the flag into a curve. The waves in the flag are shaped by the vortices travelling along it. If there were no vortices, a flag would stick straight out in the wind without flapping at all.

- A tornado is a very large vortex with air spinning around so fast (600 km/h, or 373 mph) that the air in the centre is pulled outward, creating extremely low pressure. There is literally a hole in the centre of a tornado, similar to the hole in the water going down the drain. This low pressure can suck air out of buildings so quickly that the buildings explode outward.

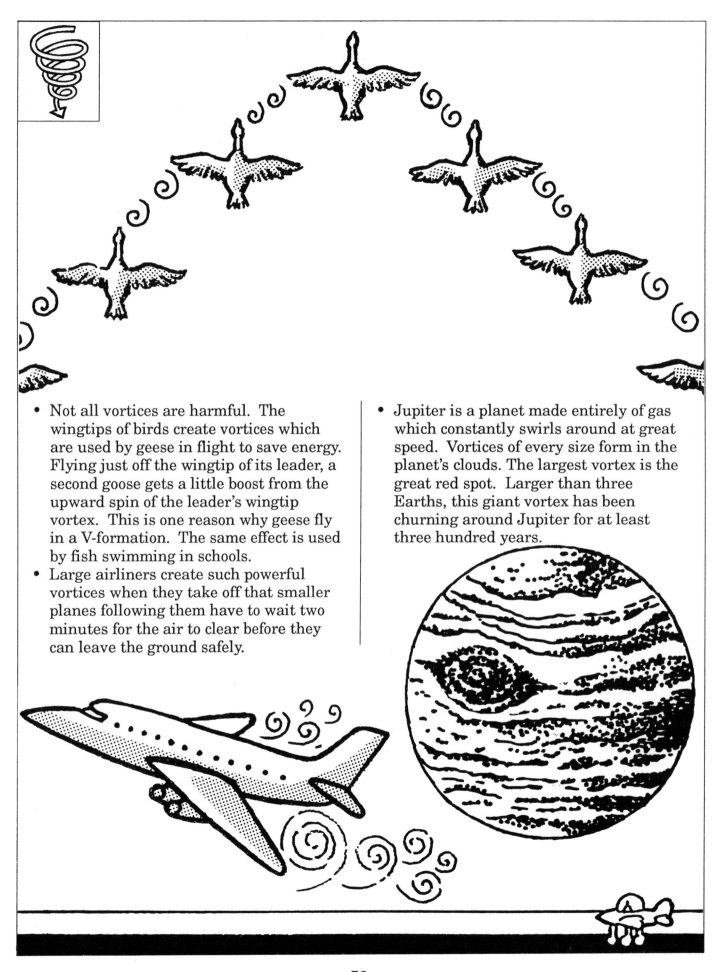

- Not all vortices are harmful. The wingtips of birds create vortices which are used by geese in flight to save energy. Flying just off the wingtip of its leader, a second goose gets a little boost from the upward spin of the leader's wingtip vortex. This is one reason why geese fly in a V-formation. The same effect is used by fish swimming in schools.
- Large airliners create such powerful vortices when they take off that smaller planes following them have to wait two minutes for the air to clear before they can leave the ground safely.

- Jupiter is a planet made entirely of gas which constantly swirls around at great speed. Vortices of every size form in the planet's clouds. The largest vortex is the great red spot. Larger than three Earths, this giant vortex has been churning around Jupiter for at least three hundred years.

Why is there no gravity on the Moon

Actually there *is* gravity on the Moon, but not as much as there is on Earth. Many people believe that as soon as you leave Earth, there is no more gravity. Astronauts floating around in space give a misleading picture. Although astronauts can feel *weightless* in space, they are still under the influence of gravity.

In fact, there is no place in the entire universe where gravity is not at work. It is the most far-reaching force known.

Gravity exists whenever there is mass.

That means that your body has its own gravity. You don't feel it because your body is not very massive. You need something the size of a planet or a moon before gravity really becomes noticeable.

The Moon has less gravity than Earth because it is less massive. The gravity on the Moon is only one-sixth as strong as that on Earth. Because of this, walking becomes a different experience. You move about in large leaps rather than small steps.

A spacecraft orbiting the Earth is still being pulled by the Earth's gravity, but because it is moving at almost 40 000 km/h, it is not pulled down to the ground. There is a tug-of-war between the Earth's gravity, which tries to pull the spacecraft down, and the tendency of the spacecraft to move forward in a straight line because of its speed. If the speed is too slow, gravity wins, and the spacecraft falls. If the speed is too high, the spacecraft wins and escapes the Earth's gravity altogether, flying off into outer space. If the speed is just right, neither side wins, and the spacecraft ends up orbiting the Earth.

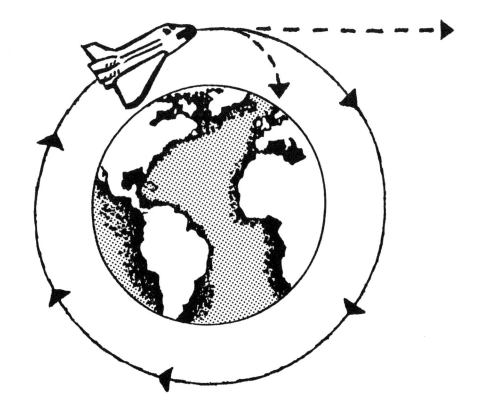

KITCHEN DEMO

Falling Objects

According to Galileo, an Italian astronomer who lived over three hundred years ago, all objects fall at the same speed, regardless of their mass. Was Galileo right?

Things you need
- heavy book
- piece of paper slightly smaller than the cover of the book

What to do
1. Hold the book and the piece of paper straight out at arm's length, one in each hand. Make sure they are both flat with respect to the floor. Drop them at the same time. Which one reaches the floor first?

2. Try dropping them again from the same height, but this time lay the piece of paper on top of the book. What happens when they fall together this time?

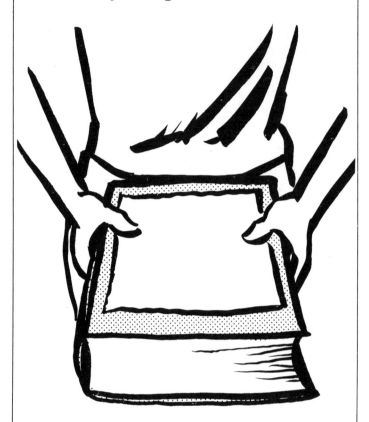

Explanation
The book and paper have different masses, but their surface areas are almost the same. When they fall, they encounter air resistance. Since the paper is lighter than the book, it is slowed more by the air resistance and takes longer to reach the floor.

When the paper is placed on top of the book, it no longer has to fight air resistance because the book pushes the air out of the way. Now both objects fall at the same speed.

The air resistance of the paper can also be reduced by crunching it up into a small ball.

If you were to drop the book and paper side by side on the Moon, where there is no air, they would both fall at the same speed. Galileo was right!

DID YOU KNOW ???

- An orbiting spacecraft is continually falling. Since all objects fall at the same speed, the spacecraft and the astronauts inside it fall together, creating the sensation of weightlessness. The floating motion is the same as that experienced by a group of skydivers all falling at the same speed.

- Phobos, a moon of Mars, has such low gravity you could pick up a rock on its surface, throw it at the horizon, and send it into orbit. About an hour and a half later, the rock would return over the opposite horizon. Can you imagine playing a game of baseball with yourself on Phobos?

- Imagine the feeling of a fall where you never hit bottom. That is the sensation astronauts feel when in orbit, which is why some develop temporary space sickness.

The interplanetary spacecraft Voyager I and II, which were launched in 1977 on a flight through the solar system are steered by the gravitational pull of the planets. Passing by Jupiter, they used the powerful gravity of the giant planet to throw the spacecraft towards Saturn.

At Saturn, Voyager II's course was changed by that planet's gravity to throw the spacecraft towards Uranus. Uranus did the same thing to throw it towards Neptune. Eventually, both Voyagers will leave our solar system altogether. They are the fastest flying objects ever constructed by humans.

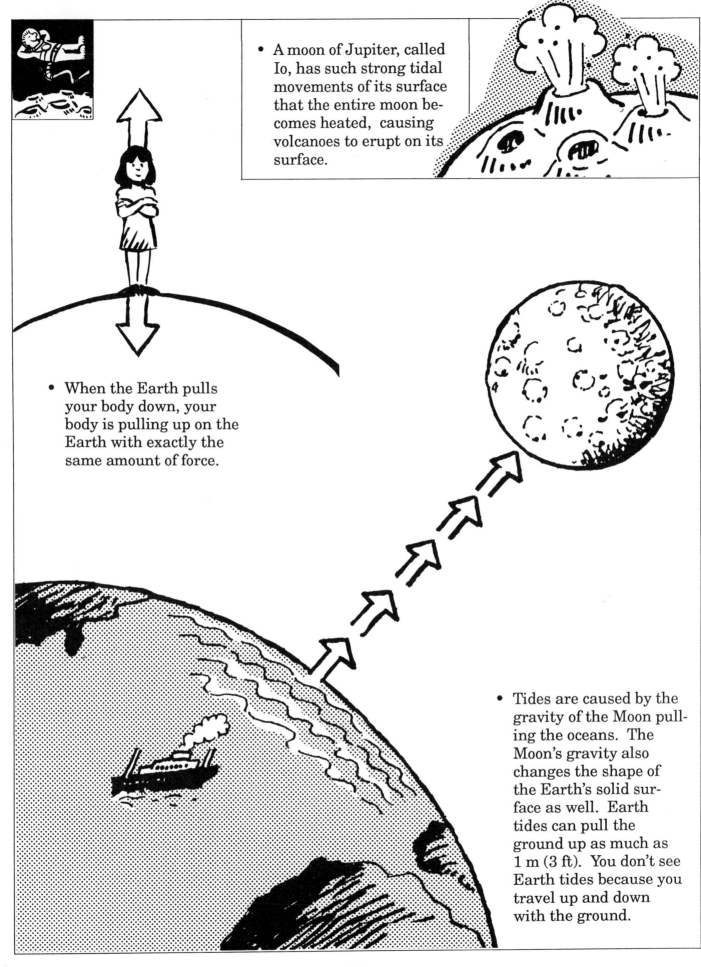

- A moon of Jupiter, called Io, has such strong tidal movements of its surface that the entire moon becomes heated, causing volcanoes to erupt on its surface.

- When the Earth pulls your body down, your body is pulling up on the Earth with exactly the same amount of force.

- Tides are caused by the gravity of the Moon pulling the oceans. The Moon's gravity also changes the shape of the Earth's solid surface as well. Earth tides can pull the ground up as much as 1 m (3 ft). You don't see Earth tides because you travel up and down with the ground.

Design an Alien

The shape of creatures on land is partly due to gravity. When humans travel in space and are exposed to low gravity, their bodies change shape slightly. Fluids shift to the upper parts of the body producing "puffy faces" and "bird legs." Spines get longer, and bones become thinner and weaker, all adaptations to weightlessness.

Choose an animal that lives on land, and redesign it for life on a planet with much lower gravity than that of Earth. Would it need large muscles and a strong skeleton?

What kinds of things could your creature do under low gravity that it cannot do on Earth?

Garbage Can Gravity Well

No one really knows how gravity works. Einstein suggested that massive objects actually curve space, so that other objects passing near them will follow the curves of this space. Here's how to build a model of Einstein's curved space.

Things you need
- plastic garbage bag
- large garbage can
- baseball
- table-tennis ball

What to do
1. Cut two sides of a plastic garbage bag to make a single sheet.
2. Stretch the sheet over the top of a large garbage can and tie it tightly to make a smooth drum. This is a model of space!

3. Place a baseball in the centre of the plastic sheet. The dent it makes represents Einstein's idea of curved space. It is called a *gravity well*.
4. Place a table-tennis ball anywhere on the surface and let it go. It will be attracted to the baseball, just as your body is attracted to the Earth. If you roll the small ball directly away from the baseball, it will fall straight back, just as an object thrown upwards falls straight back to Earth.
5. Try to orbit the small ball around the baseball. How important is the speed of the small ball? What happens if it moves too slowly?

Why are there so many craters on the Moon

The craters on the Moon were made by the same forces that created the Moon and all the planets. Some scientists believe that when our solar system began, it was nothing but a big rotating cloud of gas, dust, and dirt. As this debris drifted about, pieces of dirt would occasionally run into each other and stick together. Soon, big clumps of dirt began to form. The clumps had enough gravitational pull to actually attract other pieces of dirt, which stuck to the surfaces of the big pieces, making them grow even bigger.

Some of the clumps grew and eventually became the planets and moons. As they travelled around the newborn Sun, these larger pieces ran into the smaller pieces of dirt and dust still floating in space. Whenever a large piece of space dirt hit the surface of a planet or moon, it exploded, making a big hole, or crater, in the ground.

You cannot see many craters on Earth because Earth developed an atmosphere with wind and rain, which gradually washed the craters smooth. Earth also has vegetation which has grown over the marks, so that only the largest craters can be seen from an aircraft or from space. One of the biggest craters on Earth is the Manicouagan, now a lake in northern Quebec.

As the Moon has no atmosphere and no wind or rain, its craters remain intact today. So when you see the face of "the man in the moon," you are seeing some of the features that were formed more than two billion years ago.

KITCHEN DEMO

Create a Crater

Things you need
- large mixing bowl
- dry plaster of paris (if unavailable, use flour)
- several balls or small objects of different weights
- spray bottle filled with water

What to do
1. Cover the bottom of the bowl with the dry plaster of paris to a depth of at least 5 cm (2 in).
2. Hold one of the balls about 1 m (3 ft) over the bowl and let it drop into the powder.
3. Examine the structure of the crater made by the impact of the ball.
4. Experiment by dropping the ball from different heights, and try balls of different sizes. What affects the size of the crater?
5. Make several impacts of different sizes until they begin overlapping and old craters begin to get destroyed by new ones. When the surface of the powder begins to look like the picture of the Moon's surface, you have created a "lunar landscape."
6. When you are satisfied with your lunar landscape, gently spray the surface with a fine mist of water. Allow it to dry, and you will have a surface that is hard and ready to display. You can even paint it and build a model Moon colony on the surface.

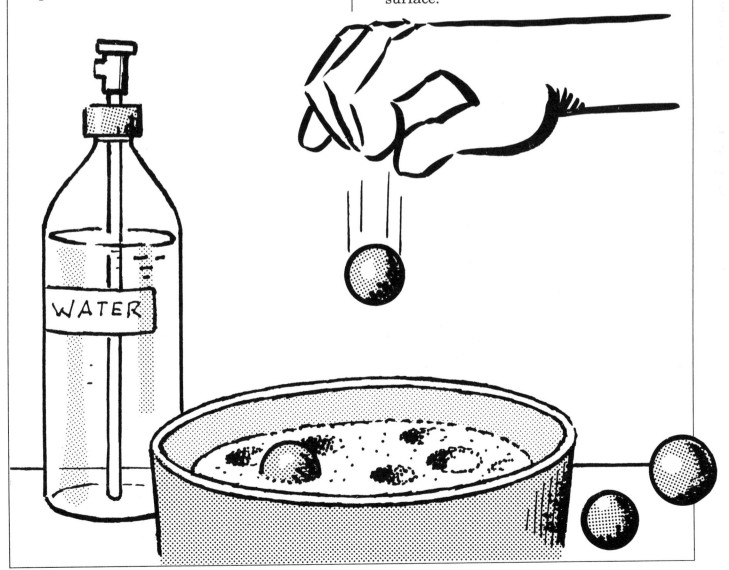

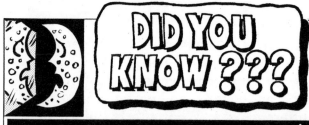

DID YOU KNOW ???

Most of the big pieces of space debris have already been swept up by the orbiting planets, but collisions between smaller particles and planets still continue. Tiny meteors collide with the Earth and the Moon every day. Most of them burn up in the Earth's atmosphere, appearing as quick flashes (shooting stars) in the night sky. On the Moon, which has no atmosphere, they reach the surface, making small craters, some only visible under a microscope.

Some scientists believe that giant meteors hitting the Earth were responsible for massive destructions of life. The last great destruction, 65 million years ago, may explain what caused the dinosaurs to become extinct. The explosion from the impact of a large meteor would be so tremendous that great dark clouds would cover the Earth for years, cooling the climate and killing off much of the life that depends on sunlight.

The theory has not been proven because no one has found a crater from a meteor that would be large enough to cause the extinction of the dinosaurs. However,

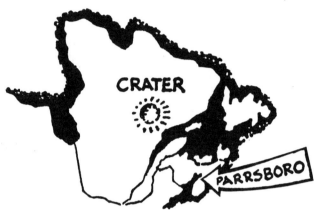

CRATER

PARRSBORO

studies being conducted in an area of Nova Scotia near Parrsboro, show an extinction that happened 200 million years ago, almost exactly the same age as the Manicouagan crater. If a link can be made between the extinction and the crater, it will be the best proof today that the impact theory of extinction may be correct.

- Space scientists can use craters to tell the age of a surface of a body in space. It is believed that most cratering stopped about three billion years ago. If there are a lot of craters, as on our Moon, the surface must be very old. If there are not many craters visible, that means something has changed the surface and covered over the old craters. The surface of the Earth, for example, is considered new, because it is constantly being changed by weather and volcanoes and there are few signs of meteor impacts.

- The side of the Moon facing the Earth is newer than the far side. The large smooth features or "seas" that make up the face of "the man in the moon" are actually craters made by meteors so large that their impact broke right through the crust of the Moon. Liquid lava oozed up from below to form a smooth surface. The far side, on the other hand, has almost no smooth surfaces, showing that not much has happened there for two billion years.

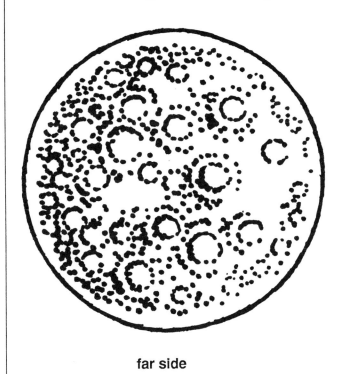

far side

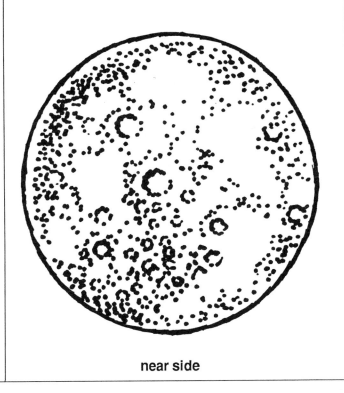

near side

When a skeleton is found, how can you tell if it was a boy or a girl

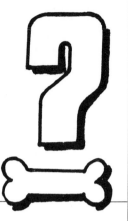

*T*here are physical differences between boys and girls, right down to our bones. Besides the general difference that girls tend to have smaller bones than boys, there is another more positive way to tell the difference.

Your hips are made of a very large bone called the *pelvis*. You can feel part of it sticking out your sides just below your waist.

The pelvic bone has a different shape in girls than it does in boys, so that females can carry and give birth to babies.

You can see that the opening in the centre of the pelvic bone is larger in the female. This is to allow the head of a baby to pass through at the time of birth. The larger pelvic bone explains why women tend to have wider hips than men.

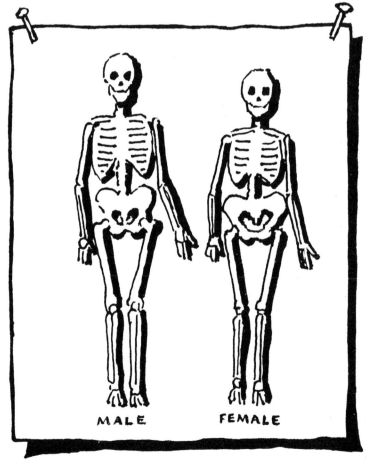

MALE   FEMALE

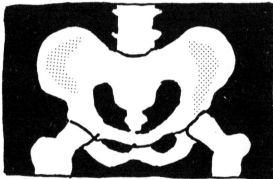

MALE

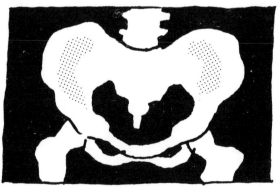

FEMALE

Body Tricks

Try these body tricks with your friends to show the difference between male and female skeletons. You may find that some people can do these activities while others cannot. The differences are greater in adults than in children below the age of physical maturity.

Things you need
- several friends (boys and girls)
- kitchen chair
- small ball or penny

What to do

1. Stand close to a wall with one foot actually touching the wall. Try to raise the other leg.

2. Place a chair against a wall. Stand facing the wall with your feet in front of the chair legs. Bend over so that your head rests on the wall. Reach down and grab the seat of the chair. Try to pick the chair up off the floor, and then stand up straight.

3. Kneel on the floor and place your elbows against your knees. Place a small ball, or a penny, on the floor between your fingertips. Straighten up, and clasp your hands behind your back. Try to touch the spot on the floor with your nose while keeping your hands behind your back.

4. Ask a friend to sit in a chair with his or her feet flat on the floor. Stand in front of the chair and press your finger on your friend's forehead. Challenge your friend to get up without pressing against your finger. Your friend will find it impossible to move – even if you are only half as big!

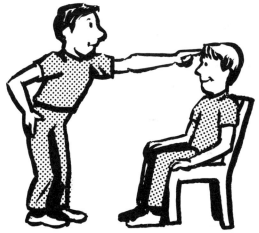

Explanation

All these body tricks are based on an imaginary point in your body called the centre of gravity. This is the point in an object where gravity seems to do all its work. In a regular-shaped body, such as a ball, the centre of gravity is usually close to the centre of the object. If the object has an irregular shape, such as the human body, the centre of gravity is in a different location for each shape.

Your centre of gravity is usually somewhere in your chest. Females tend to have a lower centre of gravity than males because

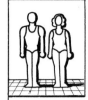

of their wider pelvic bone. This lower centre of gravity means they can sometimes perform stunts such as picking up the chair or touching their nose to the floor. A person with a higher centre of gravity has difficulty with these stunts. When such persons are bent over, the higher centre of gravity makes them lose their balance.

When you stand up straight, your centre of gravity is directly over a spot between your feet, and it is easy to keep your balance. If you stand on one foot, you have to lean to the side to move your centre of gravity over the foot still on the ground. That's why everyone has trouble when standing up against a wall. It is impossible to lift your outside leg without falling because you cannot lean over your supporting leg.

DID YOU KNOW ???

- When Dr. Donald Johanson discovered the skeleton of "Lucy," the oldest human ancestor ever found, he knew that she was a female because of the shape of the pelvic bone.

- There are only three points where an object can be supported so that it will not fall over. These are above, on, or directly below the centre of gravity. When a crane picks up a load, the cable must be directly over the centre of gravity of the load, otherwise it will spill. Construction workers learn how to position the cable so that the load can be picked up safely.

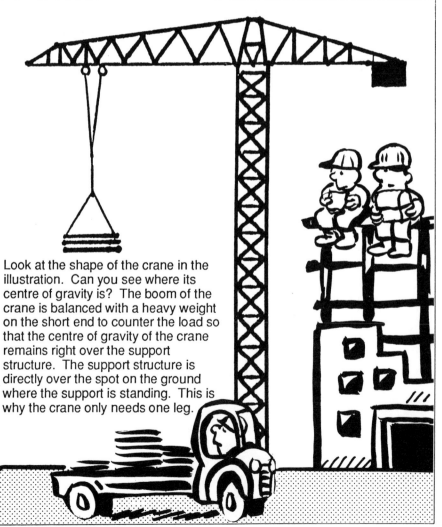

Look at the shape of the crane in the illustration. Can you see where its centre of gravity is? The boom of the crane is balanced with a heavy weight on the short end to counter the load so that the centre of gravity of the crane remains right over the support structure. The support structure is directly over the spot on the ground where the support is standing. This is why the crane only needs one leg.

- Which way would you steer to get out of this situation?

    Your instincts might tell you to turn away from the car door, but the best thing to do is to first steer *toward* the door. Why?

    Staying upright on a bicycle means keeping your centre of gravity over the wheels. When you turn, you lean your centre of gravity to one side, the bike first leans and then turns in that direction. To quickly avoid the car door, there isn't time to lean your body. By turning the wheel toward the car first, the bicycle will suddenly move out from under your body, placing your centre of gravity on the side of the wheels away from the door. If you then recover and turn the wheel away from the car, the bicycle will follow your body lean and stay under you as you swoop away from the danger.

- Good stunt riders may not know it, but their centre of gravity is always directly over the point of contact between their bike and the ground. This is the secret behind a successful "wheelie." You have to hold the bike close to your chest and think about keeping the back wheel under your chest. As long as you can hold it there, you can keep moving with the front wheel in the air.

- Have you ever wondered why a chair lift on a ski hill does not twist the cable? The support arm is attached to only one side of the chair, and hooks onto the cable from that side. But the cable does not twist because the centre of gravity of the system is a point in the chair directly below the cable. It doesn't really matter what shape the arm is, as long as the centre of gravity remains directly below the cable.

 Cut a piece of heavy cardboard into the shape shown in the picture. Place a belt in the notch as shown, and you will be able to support the holder by its end point alone. Where is the centre of gravity in this system ?

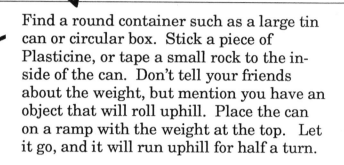

Find a round container such as a large tin can or circular box. Stick a piece of Plasticine, or tape a small rock to the inside of the can. Don't tell your friends about the weight, but mention you have an object that will roll uphill. Place the can on a ramp with the weight at the top. Let it go, and it will run uphill for half a turn.

- Knowing about the centre of gravity helped palaeontologists unravel a mystery about how some dinosaurs walked. Old drawings show the animals standing upright, with their tails dragging on the ground. But a study of the way the hip bones fit into the pelvic bones showed that the animals could not stand that way without suffering a lot of pain. The drawings were revised to show a more stooped-over position. In order to keep the centre of gravity over their feet in this position, the animals had to hold their massive tails straight out behind for balance. This new position means that such animals, once thought to be slow-moving, were actually quite fast for their size.

Why does the shower curtain bend inward when the shower is turned on

When the water shoots out of the shower head, it carries some of the air inside the shower down with it. The moving air on the inside of the shower curtain creates a lower pressure than the still air on the outside. The outside air pushes inward because its pressure is greater.

The discovery that fast-moving air creates low pressure was made by a scientist named Daniel Bernoulli. This effect, called the Bernoulli principle, is responsible not only for moving your shower curtain, but also for keeping birds and airplanes in the air, for creating the curve of a baseball, and for drawing the smoke out of a chimney.

There are also times when the effect is a nuisance, such as when tall buildings produce strong winds in the streets below.

When low-speed winds pass through the narrow gap between tall skyscrapers, the air speeds up, just as a river speeds up when it passes through a narrow gorge. Pedestrians have to battle strong winds in the gap between the buildings, while there may be almost no wind a short distance away. During storms, these narrow gaps can create dangerously high winds. Engineers designing cities try to avoid gaps like these so that pedestrians will not have to fight such winds, which can appear even on calm days.

Levitation Trick

Have you ever tried to make a ball rise up in the air without touching it?

Things you need
- plastic drinking straw (the kind that bends)
- 2 or 3 table tennis balls
- vacuum cleaner
- hair dryer

What to do
1. Hold the straw straight up and down and hold the table tennis ball directly over the upper end.
2. Blow hard and steady through the bottom of the straw and let go of the ball. If you blow hard enough, the ball will remain suspended over the end of the straw.

3. A less tiring way is to use a vacuum cleaner with the hose attached to the exhaust, so the air blows outward. You can also use a hand-held hair dryer.

   Tilt the vacuum hose slightly while the ball is raised up, or levitated, and watch what happens. How far to the side can you tilt the hose? Try adding more table tennis balls and see how many you can levitate at the same time.

Explanation
The fast-moving air from the straw or blower creates lower pressure than the surrounding air. The ball is held in the airstream by the higher pressure of the surrounding air. This pressure is strong enough to hold the ball when the airstream is at an angle. If the angle is too great, the force of gravity will pull the ball out of the low pressure area and the ball will fall.

- The Bernoulli principle is used by airplanes to help create lift. The upper surfaces of the wings are curved so that the air moving over the top of the wing has to move faster than the air that goes under the wing. This creates lower pressure on top, which helps lift the wing into the air.

   The next time you see the shower curtains curve inward when you turn the water on, remember that the same effect helps to lift jumbo jets into the air!

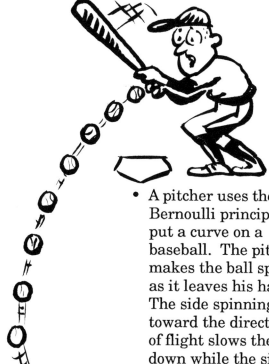

- A pitcher uses the Bernoulli principle to put a curve on a baseball. The pitcher makes the ball spin as it leaves his hand. The side spinning toward the direction of flight slows the air down while the side spinning backwards speeds the air up. The faster air creates lower pressure on that side of the ball, so the ball curves towards the low pressure side. Pitchers can use this to cause the ball to curve left, curve right, drop, or even lift, in an attempt to fool the batter.

92

- Prairie dogs use the Bernoulli principle to cool their tunnels. A mound of dirt around the entrance to the tunnel causes the air to speed up as it passes over. This creates an area of lower pressure over the hole, which draws air out of the tunnel like a fan. The opening at the other end of the tunnel does not have a mound, so the air will flow through the tunnel from one end to the other, rather than be drawn out both ends at the same time.

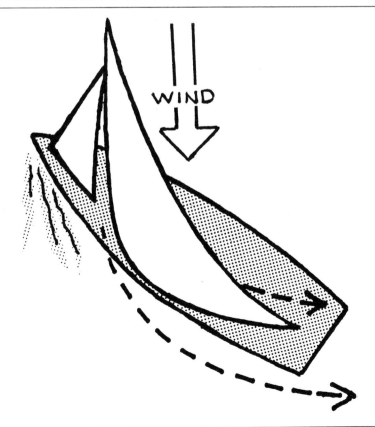

WIND

- A sailboat is like an airplane moving sideways. As air passes around the curved surface of a sail, it moves more quickly around the front side than around the back. This lowers the pressure so the sail is actually pulled through the air. This is why a sailboat moves fastest when it is travelling across the wind rather than being blown in the same direction as the wind.

The Flyaway, an amusement ride in St-Simone, Quebec, uses a giant fan and the Bernoulli principle to suspend people in midair!

You can amaze your friends by appearing to blow out a candle through a bottle. Simply hold the bottle directly between your mouth and the flame, then blow. As the air passes around the curved sides of the bottle, it speeds up. The lower air pressure keeps your breath attached to the sides of the bottle longer. This allows the split airstream to join together again on the backside of the bottle and continue with enough force to blow out the candle.

Do scientists have all the answers ?

Good science is good questions, but scientists don't always have the answers. If you had fun exploring the questions in this book, here are a few more to ponder, questions that science has no answers to:

Why do some people sneeze when they look at the Sun?

Why do you feel like yawning when someone else yawns?

What started the "Big Bang" that started the whole universe?

How does a single fertilized cell know how to reproduce itself into trillions of different cells that make up a human body?

How do we remember?

What did dinosaurs sound like?

Was there ever life on Mars?

How does gravity work?

Index